GUIDES TO OFFICIAL PUBLICATIONS
Volume 10
Editor: John E. Pemberton, University College at Buckingham, England

AN INTRODUCTION TO JAPANESE GOVERNMENT PUBLICATIONS

GUIDES TO OFFICIAL PUBLICATIONS

AN INTRODUCTION TO JAPANESE GOVERNMENT PUBLICATIONS

by
TSUTOMU KUROKI
Assistant Professor, National College of Library Science, Japan

Translated by
MASAKO KISHI

with an annotated bibliography by
CHINE HAYESHI

PERGAMON PRESS
OXFORD · NEW YORK · TORONTO · SYDNEY · PARIS · FRANKFURT

U.K.	Pergamon Press Ltd., Headington Hill Hall, Oxford OX3 0BW, England
U.S.A.	Pergamon Press Inc., Maxwell House, Fairview Park, Elmsford, New York 10523, U.S.A.
CANADA	Pergamon Press Canada Ltd., Suite 104, 150 Consumers Rd., Willowdale, Ontario M2J 1P9, Canada
AUSTRALIA	Pergamon Press (Aust.) Pty. Ltd., P.O. Box 544, Potts Point, N.S.W. 2011, Australia
FRANCE	Pergamon Press SARL, 24 rue des Ecoles, 75240 Paris, Cedex 05, France
FEDERAL REPUBLIC OF GERMANY	Pergamon Press GmbH, 6242 Kronberg-Taunus, Hammerweg 6, Federal Republic of Germany

Copyright © 1981 Pergamon Press Ltd.

All Rights Reserved. No part of this publication may be reproduced, stored in a retrieval system or transmitted in any form or by any means: electronic, electrostatic, magnetic tape, mechanical, photocopying, recording or otherwise, without permission in writing from the publishers.

First English edition 1981

British Library Cataloguing in Publication Data

Kuroki, Tsutomu
An introduction to Japanese government publications.
- (Guides to official publications; vol. 10).
1. Japan - Government publications - Bibliography
I. Title II. Series
015'.52   Z3305   80-41735
ISBN 0 08 024679 6

First published in Japan by Gyosei Ltd., under the title SEIFU KANKOBUTSU GAISETSU by Tsutomu Kuroki
© 1972 Tsutomu Kuroki

In order to make this volume available as economically and as rapidly as possible the author's typescript has been reproduced in its original form. This method unfortunately has its typographical limitations but it is hoped that they in no way distract the reader.

Printed in Great Britain by A. Wheaton & Co. Ltd., Exeter

AUTHOR'S PREFACE

Nowadays we receive a variety of information through newspapers, magazines, books, radio and television, but the amount put out by the government is especially voluminous and diverse. Government publications are very important and constitute fundamental data in being able to research and understand the current conditions of, for example, politics, economics, society, education and culture.

So far, in our country, government publications have not been well used, due partly to lack of public interest and partly to the limited number of publications which in any case are sometimes not available to the public. Recently, however, as their significance has been recognized and the means of publishing and distributing them have been improved, demand is increasing.

As a result of the nature of my work, I have often been asked about material in government publications and have had to answer students, researchers and others from my incomplete knowledge or from experience. I, therefore, felt strongly that some kind of manual of government publications was needed. Unfortunately, no systematic introduction to government publications has so far been published which adequately meets the differing demands of research.

In this book, therefore, I have tried to explain the contents and characteristics of government publications. I sincerely hope that this will not only help librarians but also researchers, students and laymen.

It is a very difficult task to grasp the entire scope of government publications. I sometimes became discouraged in view of the volume and variety of information printed and in the reali-

zation of how complicated government organizations really are.
At such times, however, the achievements of my predecessors have
encouraged and helped me. It is my wish to continue improving
this guide with the help of readers, comments and suggestions.

Finally I wish to give special thanks to Mr. Narau Okuda,
President of the Japan Society of Library Science, who has given
me every encouragement. I would also like to say a sincere
thank you to Professor Kintaro Hattori for his valuable advice,
to Professor Masanori Ishizuka who gave me the necessary inspira-
tion and to Professor Seiichi Kitero for his priceless instruction through the Seminar on Reference Work.

I greatly value the efforts and care of Mr. Tomomaso Ogawa of
Gyosei Ltd., Publishers, in publishing this work, which is my
first publication.

CONTENTS

PART I
STRUCTURE OF GOVERNMENT PUBLICATIONS

Chapter 1. ORIGIN AND FLOW OF GOVERNMENT
PUBLICATIONS   3

    1. History of Government Publications   3
    2. Official Gazette   6
    3. Government Publications at Present   15

       Government Publications from a
       Statistical Viewpoint   15

       Use and General Knowledge of
       Government Publications from a
       Statistical Viewpoint   17

Chapter 2. DEFINITION OF GOVERNMENT
PUBLICATIONS   22

Chapter 3. TYPES AND CHARACTERISTICS OF
GOVERNMENT PUBLICATIONS   27

    1. Types of Government Publications   27
    2. Characteristics of Government
       Publications   30
    3. White Paper   35

       History   36

       Outline   39

Chapter 4. PRODUCTION PROCEDURE AND
AUTHORSHIP OF GOVERNMENT
PUBLICATIONS   45

1. Production Procedure of Government
   Publications   45
2. Public Relations of Government Organ-
   izations   48
       Outline   48
       Public Relations' Mechanism in the
       Ministry and Agency   50
       Central Public Relations Organization   53
       Publicity Media and Government Pub-
       lications   55
3. Government Statistics   58
       Statistical Researches and Government
       Offices' Statistics   58
       Statistical System of Our Country   60
       Designated Statistics System   65
       Notified Statistics System   68
       Statistical Reports Coordination
       System   70
4. Government Publications and Copyright   72
       Works of Government Organizations   73
       Author of the Government Publications   75
       Exploitation of the Works of the
       Government Organizations   77

PART II
PUBLICATION AND DISTRIBUTION OF
GOVERNMENT PUBLICATIONS

Chapter 1. PUBLISHING ORGANIZATIONS OF
            GOVERNMENT PUBLICATIONS   85
       1. Publication of the Government Publica-
          tions in Europe and the U.S.   85

2. The Publishing of Government Publications in Japan   88
3. Printing Bureau of the Ministry of
   Finance   92

   History of the Printing Bureau of the
   Ministry of Finance   92

   Development of the Publishing   92

Chapter 2. DISTRIBUTION OF GOVERNMENT
   PUBLICATIONS   98

1. The Structure of Government Publications
   Distribution   98
2. The Diffusion and Sales Organizations of
   Government Publications   100

   History   100

   Current Conditions of Diffusion and
   Sales   105

3. Organizations that Collect and Offer
   Government Publications   106
   Outline   106

   Deposit Copy System in Japan   107

   Organizations Offering Services for
   Government Publication Users   110

PART III
RETRIEVAL OF GOVERNMENT PUBLICATIONS

1. Method of Government Publications
   Retrieval   117
2. General Bibliography for Government
   Publications   119
3. Bibliography for Each Government
   Office   121
4. Trade Bibliography   124

PART IV
ANNOTATIONS OF GOVERNMENT
PUBLICATIONS

Introductory Remarks   129

Chapter 1. PERIODICALS   130

Chapter 2. WHITE PAPER   142

Chapter 3. INVESTIGATIONS, STATISTICS,
REPORTS, etc.   154

APPENDICES

Appendix 1. Agreement Concerning the Treatment of
Government Publications (White Paper, etc.)   185

Appendix 2. Regulations of the Council of the Diffusion of
Government Publications   188

Appendix 3. Agreement of the Council of the Diffusion of
Government Publications   191

Appendix 4. List of the Designated Statistics   194

INDEX   201

PART I

STRUCTURE OF GOVERNMENT PUBLICATIONS

CHAPTER 1
ORIGIN AND FLOW OF GOVERNMENT PUBLICATIONS

1.   History of Government Publications

In a democratic system of government political decisions should
be based on the consent of the people. As a result the people
need to be aware both of their rights and obligations in ensuring
that their opinions are properly reflected by the administrators.
Communication between people and government is, therefore, of
great importance in order that the people may become familiar
with government policy. One vital method of communication is
through government publications.

Japanese government publications have, through the ages, exerted
a considerable influence in such areas as politics, economics
and culture. In their development they have undergone great
changes, sometimes being known as the *Imperial Bulletin*
(Chokuhan) and sometimes as the *Official Bulletin* (Kanpan).
They are said to date back to the time when politics itself
began. It is, however, generally agreed that the *Journal of the
Cabinet* (Dajokan Nisshi) is the forefather of modern government
publications. This was first published in Kyoto on the 23rd
February, 1867 (4th year of Keio)* just before the advent of
the Meiji era. The *Journal of the Cabinet* was a bulletin which
the restoration government published in order to spread its
policies and disseminate information. This was done to gain
the support of the various feudal clans and common people. It
also served as a public relations magazine in that it published,
among other things, the new Meiji Government's policies and
current information on feudal uprisings.

At first Kanbe-e Murakami (a government patronized publisher in
Kyoto) was responsible for publishing the *Journal of the
Cabinet*. Before long, however, Mohe-e Suwaraya (a government-
patronized publisher in Tokyo) took over. At this time it

contained several pages of half a sheet of rice paper and was
published irregularly. The first issue contained seven sheets
of rice paper and it is said that it took only two hours for
fifty craftsmen to engrave the printing plates. The Printing
Bureau eventually took the lead in typographic methods.

Following the Cabinet's example, each Ministry began to publish
its own journal. Major examples include the *Journal of the
Ministry of Foreign Affairs*, *Journal of the Ministry of Communication and Construction*, *Journal of the Ministry of Education*,
Journal of the Ministry of War, *Journal of the Ministry of
Justice*, *Journal of the Ministry of Home Affairs* and *Journal of
the Ministry of the Navy*. At this time the number of Journals
reached thirty. On the 2nd July, 1877 the *Journal of the
Cabinet* was discontinued, to be replaced on the 2nd July, 1883
by the *Official Gazette*. By this time the journals published
by each Ministry also began to cease publication and were all
eventually united into the *Official Gazette* (Kanpo).

Now let us look at the changes in government publications
against the background of the times throughout the Meiji (1867-
1912), Taisho (1912-1926) and Showa (1926-   ) eras. Governmental publications in the early Meiji era consisted mainly of
laws and regulations, translations of works of art, science and
culture from foreign countries and histories of government
offices. The new government, in trying to outgrow its former
self and shape a modern country, felt an urgent need to
establish a governmental system that would promulgate and enforce the law, and set down guidelines for the organization of
the new administration. Commercial newspapers were at that
time underdeveloped and as a result a bulletin which would
disseminate the large number of laws and regulations was badly
needed. Meanwhile, foreign books on laws, institutions,
science and culture were extensively translated into Japanese
so that the people could use them as models, examine and
imitate them. Science and culture as characteristics of the
early stage of Europeanization were developed from this point on.

The Ministries of War, the Navy, Agriculture and Commerce, and
Education were very active in publishing, especially the
Ministry of Education. From 1871-1873 fifty-two items which
can be subdivided into ninety-one volumes and forty-four
volumes of edited compilations were published. Other Ministries
also published quite a large number of translations in comparison
to other works, as is shown by the *Catalogue of Translations of
the Ministries and Agencies* published by the Cabinet Archives

Bureau in October 1889, which lists a total of 1500 translated items. The purpose of this catalogue was to prevent duplicate translation by listing the unpublished translations of each Ministry. During this period each Ministry wholeheartedly and enthusiastically engaged in publishing translations.

The Government thought that the compilation of history was of paramount importance, especially in regard to the history of the present administration. Work was, therefore, started on compiling history very early in the Meiji restoration. As a result the following historical records were published: the *History of Money in Great Japan* published by the Ministry of Finance, the *Diplomatic Chronicle* by the Ministry of Foreign Affairs and the *History of War* by the Ministry of War. Besides these publications official business reports, annual reports, statistical research reports and stenographic records of the inauguration of the Diet were published.

By this time nearly all of the major annual administrative reports, such as the *Report of the Ministry of Agriculture and Commerce* were appearing regularly. As the structure developed, the organization of government statistical research became better established and the purposes of government publications began to be fulfilled. This is shown by the statistical research put out by the government in such works as *Company Statistics* in 1893 and *Factory Statistics* in 1909.

Government organizations have, therefore, played a significant role in the history of modern publishing. The foundations were laid in the early Meiji era when the Government took over the task of printing and publishing and each Ministry actively contributed to the output. The Ministry of Education contributed most to publishing, it established the Editorial Bureau which edited and reissued, among other things, texts, translations and dictionaries. One of the three best sellers in the Keiji era was the *Outline of Geography* which was written by Masao Uchida and put out as an official publication. The *Encyclopaedia* (1884–1885) which was, the translation of Chambers' *Information for the people*, is also very well known. In addition they published a Japanese *Lexicon (Genkai)* manuscript by Fumihiko Otsuki, a *Bibliographical Dictionary of Great Japan*, and republished *Gunshoruiju*. They also undertook the immense task of publishing the *Encyclopaedia of Allied Works (Kojiruien)* from 1879 to 1890, though it was not completed until 1914. The Ministry of Agriculture and Commerce was similarly active in publishing. According to the *Ministry of Agriculture and*

Commerce Publication List, issued in 1899, there were 1,477
publications by that Ministry during the period from its establishment in July 1881 until March 1899.

At the time of the Taisho era government publications developed
and became rich in content, the best example of this being the
first National Population census taken in 1920. Although the
Statistics Bureau did conduct a census in Kai Province in 1879,
the 1920 census was the first national census. Throughout the
long period taken for Japan to develop into a modern country,
the national census was an indication of the modernization
achieved and of Japanese progress towards becoming a great power.
Under the Taisho democracy everyone was in high spirits and
against this background of modernization government publications
were obliged to improve and the *Official Gazette,* the primary
government publication, made considerable improvement in content.
It was also necessary for other various types of publications
to change with the times.

At the advent of the Showa era Japan was adversely affected by
Imperialism. For a while it seemed that the goal of government
publications, which is to report the true facts of a situation,
was almost lost.

After the war official publications were best put to use as a
generative power for establishing democracy much in the same
way as the Meiji had previously used them to establish their
own form of government. Both the Showa government and the
people now realized the importance of government publications
as a medium of communication.

2.   Official Gazette

In the previous section the publication of the *Official Gazette*
(Kanpo) was discussed. The term "official gazette" has been
used for government publications through the years. In this
time it has been a mainstay in the development of these publications and it is, therefore, worthwhile to look at the changes
which have occurred.

The *Journal of the Cabinet,* founded on 23rd February, 1867 was
used to diffuse government policy and propaganda in order to
help stabilize the country. In The Notification (Ose Idegaki)
of April 5th, 1867 reference is made to the purpose of the
Journal of the Cabinet saying, "it is intended that the ordin-

ances and announcements be widely publicized in order to reach
from rich to poor and from the upper to the lower classes, so
that all classes of people would be aware of them and would
respectfully cooperate with the Government in carrying them out".
Judging from this the primary object of the *Journal* was obviously the dissemination of laws and regulations. What is not
mentioned, however, is that it was also used as a propaganda
magazine for the purpose of defence against anti-government
groups who were setting forth their arguments in the *Chugai
Newspaper* and the like.

The *Journal* was published irregularly; at first it had a circulation of five hundred, but by 1874 it had increased nearly
threefold to 1,450. By January 1877 circulation had jumped to
6,600, but after the ninetieth volume it was assumed to have
completed its original purpose and was discontinued. In total
1,177 issues were published.

During the seven years prior to the foundation of the *Official
Gazette* the Government did not have any official organization
which proclaimed ordinances, laws and regulations, but published
them in the column "Articles and Official Bulletin of the
Cabinet" in the *Tokyo Nichi-Nichi Shinbun (Tokyo Daily Newspaper)*. The situation and circumstances at the time of the
discontinuation of the *Journal* have not been ascertained. No
official records declaring the discontinuation have been found,
except for the statement in the archives of the Printing Bureau
which reads "the *Journal of the Cabinet* has ceased to be printed
and distributed since 1877". It is argued that the Government
used the *Tokyo Daily Newspaper* because they had not decided what
to publish in place of the *Journal*.

In the announcement that the Government sent to the Tokyo Daily
Newspaper Nippo Company in regard to the column they were going
to use in the newspaper, they said that "the Government believes
that there ought to be some kind of official newspaper". From
this it is indisputable that they had been considering a Government Newspaper. It also shows that they had this idea at an
earlier time because the announcement was dated 18th October,
1877.

Eager statesmen had been strongly urging publication of a govern-
ment organ from 1877 until 1883 when finally the *Official
Gazette* was launched. In these circumstances the Cabinet
Councillor Aritomo Yamagata submitted a representation to the
Premier Sanemi Sanjo, in 1882. It was this representation which

led to the publication of the *Official Gazette*. Yamagata
stated "the Government must make the public aware of its policy
by spreading it widely and must guide the public's steps correctly concerning the basis of its policies. For this purpose,
the publication of a new kind of newspaper is the best possible
means and the most effective. It should preferably be the
combination of an official gazette and a private paper. The
official gazette is the bulletin that publishes the policies
and ideas of the Government and which is put out by the Government. The private paper is a newspaper published by a commercial company with the support and patronage of the Government
in order to mould public opinion. The cheaper the price the
better but the actual cost should be charged. It should publish
full particulars of all the Cabinet orders and ordinances,
explain the purpose and effect of the law in detail, and publish
anything relating to state policies that the Government wishes
to disseminate among the public. It should also correct any
mistakes and misunderstanding of the facts found in other
general newspapers and publicize the intention of the Government
with respect to political problems both inside and outside the
country. The official gazette should only be intended to bring
Government policies to light and therefore should not carry
editorials and the like which lead to discussion or argument.
That is the outline of the official gazette. The proposal of
the Cabinet Councillor Okura which suggests the publication of
a journal issuing the laws and ordinances has already been
passed. Its idea and aim are similar to the official gazette.
However, as the articles it would carry are limited to the laws
and regulations, it would not extend as far as to earnestly
publicize the principles and policy of the Government and guide
the people correctly. Obviously its result would not be at all
equal to that of the official gazette. I firmly request that
you reject the journal of the laws and regulations and instead
publish the official gazette proposed here. After further
consideration I shall state separately my opinion on how to
publish the official gazette. I sincerely hope that the Government will publish the official gazette most promptly and that
together with the private paper it will set people to rights,
so that the Government will not be criticized or condemned
for its indecisiveness". In short, he stressed the need for the
publication of an official gazette which would proclaim and
publish the ordinances, laws and regulations and of the govern-
ment-patronized paper which would spread the policies, inten-
tions, circumstances and views of the Government among the
public.

As a result of the discussion in regard to this representation, the Government compromised between an official gazette and the journal of ordinances, the proposal of the Cabinet Councillor Okuma, which had already passed the Cabinet. According to the record on the subject of publication of the *Official Gazette* dated 1st November, 1882, the compromise was as follows:

I.   The establishment of the Bureau of the Official Gazette within the Cabinet.

        1. The Bureau shall consist of the Director-General and the administrative officials of the Cabinet under the supervision of the Cabinet Councillors.

        2. The Bureau shall proclaim and publish the established ordinances, explain the laws and regulations, compile the reports of diplomatic establishments abroad and publish the *Official Gazette* every day.

        3. The Bureau shall either entrust the printing of the *Official Gazette* to the Printing Bureau or establish a printing office within the Cabinet to print and publish it.

        4. The Bureau shall instruct and supervise the semi-official newspaper (the regular newspaper patronized by the Government). They shall see that the newspaper makes Government policy known to the public, explain the basis of the enactment of ordinances, correct the misconceptions of public opinion and lead the public to co-operate with the Government.

        5. The Bureau shall prepare an estimate for the *Official Gazette* and appropriate a budget for it. (added in annexed paper)

        6. The *Official Gazette* shall publish the proceedings of the Council of GENRO and also state a reason for any corrections made.

        7. The *Official Gazette* shall publish the budget and the statement of accounts.

        8. Foreign news appearing in the *Official Gazette* shall be extracted only from the current issues of

official gazettes published by foreign governments.

The earlier issues of the *Official Gazette* had rather a newspaper, PR bulletin appearance. This was not only because of the
intention of the Government in relation to a government newspaper but also, and mainly, because of the demands of the times.
In 1886 the Government made a contract with Reuter's News Agency
for the receipt of foreign news under its Europeanization
policy, for at that time foreign news was inaccessible in Japan.
Accordingly, the *Official Gazette* then established a column for
foreign news and published articles on the politics, economics
and society of other countries, which were acquired from the
foreign news telegram.

Basically the *Official Gazette* was similar in character to the
organ which published the laws and regulations on the basis of
the authority of Cabinet Ordinance No. 22 of May 1883. This
prescribed that official notices and announcements should be
official only when published in the *Official Gazette*. Later,
in December 1885, ordinances and decrees were included in this
category. With the Imperial Ordinance No. 1 of 26th February,
1886 the Government established the Official Document System.
Eventually in Imperial Ordinance No. 6 of 1st February, 1907
they established the Promulgation of Laws and Regulations
System which prescribed that all laws and regulations should be
proclaimed in the *Official Gazette*.

Because the primary purpose of the *Official Gazette* was the
proclamation of laws and regulations, every journal that had
been published by each Ministry was discontinued and the pro-
clamations brought together into the *Official Gazette*.

Since its first appearance the *Official Gazette* has developed
sometimes more as a newspaper and sometimes more as a PR
bulletin. However, overall the basic theme of an organ pro-
claiming laws and regulations has been both retained and in
fact given priority. Besides the main issue, they published a
supplement and an extra edition in order to increase and enrich
the content. The "general news column" established in the
Taisho era purposely had more PR type of information in order to
attract attention. This "general news column" soon turned into
the *Weekly* that was put out separately as a supplement to the
Official Gazette; and as it carried more and more PR and propaganda material it finally developed into an independent PR
magazine.

The circulation of the *Official Gazette* showed a sharp increase
in the period from its inception in 1883 to 1891 and has been
settled since then. In the early Showa era, the National Mobilization Law was enacted and then one law after another affected
directly or indirectly by this law was promulgated. Accordingly,
at one time the *Official Gazette* was in such great demand that
the circulation went up to over 150,000 in 1943. However, as
the tide of war grew strained and the situation with regard to
materials became worse, it was reduced to around 55,000 towards
the end of the war, in May 1945. After the war on account of
the many laws and ordinances, starting from the Price Control
Ordinance, demand increased considerably resulting in a circulation of 85,000 at the end of 1947. Nevertheless demand still
exceeded supply and there was strong pressure for an increase.
Finally, in December 1947, a "Petition concerning the Increase
in Circulation of the *Official Gazette*" was submitted to the
Director-General of the Printing Bureau by the Official Gazette
Sales Stands throughout the country. As the Printing Bureau
was greatly concerned at this situation it submitted a "Petition
concerning the Additional Printing of the *Official Gazette*" to
the second Diet. Though the Diet adopted this petition they
had a very hard time maintaining the desired circulation, for
there were scarcely any materials, especially important being a
shortage of paper. Nevertheless, they increased the circulation
of 88,000 of 1947 to the post-war record of 100,000. As social
conditions became stable after the war, the demand for the
Official Gazette started to decrease. In 1953 it was down to
60,000 and by 1959 was only 45,000.

As they had never before encountered such a situation, the
authorities were perplexed at the way the circulation of the
Official Gazette tended to decrease annually. The following
are the potential reasons for the decline:

1. With the abolition of the Old Cabinet System and the
    Ordinance concerning Promulgation of Laws and Regu-
    lations, which was the authoritative law in this
    area, the *Official Gazette* lost its mission and
    basis as the organ for promulgation of laws and
    regulations.

2. The Towns and Villages Amalgamation Promotion Law
    hastened the amalgamation of the Municipalities
    and the market was reduced accordingly.

3. PR activities in the ministries and agencies
    increased.

4. Because of the retrenchment of expenditure of both
    the national and local governments, the number of
    purchasers went down.

5. The appearance of the English version in 1946
    obliged the *Official Gazette* to curtail its
    articles and insertions, which eventually reduced
    the potential value, usefulness and uniqueness of
    the content.

Special mention should be made of the post-war publication of
the English version of the *Official Gazette*. With the memorandum of the Supreme Commander of the Allied Powers received
on 15th March, 1946 they were ordered to publish 300 issues of
the English version of the *Official Gazette* each day and were
to submit them to the General Headquarters of the Allied Powers.
As the Printing Bureau was still not restored to normal operations, they foresaw the extreme difficulty in issuing the
English version under such circumstances, therefore, they were
required to urge the printing company's co-operation even in
publishing the Japanese version. They, therefore, decided to
curtail and abridge the articles of the *Official Gazette* in
order to cope with this problem. This eventually led the
Official Gazette to become a tasteless and uninteresting publication. At any rate, the first English version of the *Official
Gazette* was put out on 4th April, 1946.

Another current problem is that because of the abolition of the
Promulgation Ordinance (the authoritative law for promulgating
the laws and regulations) the promulgating system in Japan is
very obscure and indefinite. Let us look briefly at the circumstances of its abolition. Publication of the *Official Gazette*
up to World War II developed together with the promulgation of
the laws and regulations system. When the New Constitution was
established, it was expected that some measure similar to the
Promulgation Ordinance, which was established on the basis of
the Imperial Constitution of the Meiji, would be re-enacted in
it. Nonetheless, as there appeared no legislative measures for
it at the time of the enforcement of the Constitution of Japan,
with Ordinance No. 4 [the "Ordinance concerning the Abolition of
the Old Cabinet System" of 3rd May, 1947] the abolition of the
Promulgation Ordinance was made official. It meant the loss
of the legal basis for the *Official Gazette* as the official

organ for promulgating laws and regulations. In practice,
however, the decision by the Grand Bench of the Supreme Court
on 15th October, 1958, prescribed that the judicial precedent
that covers the promulgation of the laws should in principle be
effected by the *Official Gazette*. Consequently the *Official
Gazette* was deemed as having a role without a legal basis.

In the long history of the *Official Gazette* no reform bill had
ever before been submitted in such an air of crisis. After the
peak in 1949 circulation showed a steady annual decline. Moreover, as it appeared to be not a temporary but a long term
phenomenon the Printing Bureau finally had to take some action.
In October 1954 they abolished the "Matter concerning the
Curtailment of the Articles in the *Official Gazette*" because
they realized that the curtailment resulting from the publication
of the English version had made its content dull and constricted.
But they also realized that such passive action would not help
much. Therefore, on 21st November, 1955 they sent the notice
"About the Reform of the *Official Gazette*", agreed by the Council
of Vice-Ministers, to each Ministry and Agency, which was soon
given effect. Its purpose was to remedy the editing of the
Official Gazette. In order to help it work better they developed
the "Doubling of the *Official Gazette* Movement", mobilizing the
Official Gazette Sales Co-operative Association and all the
Local Sales Agencies for the *Official Gazette*. Despite this
big promotion activity and the reform of editing they did not
obtain good results. Though they intended to enrich the content
with more PR-type information it was incomparable to the immense
quantity of information sent out by the mass media. The public
had been constantly getting a great deal of accurate and current
information on the Government necessary for their daily life
through television, radio and newspaper, thanks to the development of new agencies and of social change in general. Besides
the introduction of the new aspect of PR and its development,
each Ministry was now very actively promoting PR work. Under
such circumstances, however, they were apparently not rewarded
with good results. The actual change in content also burdened
every Government organization with the added responsibility of
supplying information in addition to their own PR work. As a
result, they could not contribute as much as they hoped to.

Above all, however, the abolition of the Promulgation Ordinance
is thought to be the main cause of the decline. They would not
have gained any more distributors despite their more popular
style and content, for they did not furnish the public with
useful and practical information. This raises another problem

to think over with respect to the flexibility of the *Official Gazette* in meeting the needs of the times.

Another characteristic of the post-war *Official Gazette* is that they published the *Commentary* as a bi-weekly supplement. *The Photo* and *Current Movement: a Window on the Government* - the Government PR magazines - had branched out from this *Commentary*. It is interesting that we find a similar instance in the *Weekly*, which grew out of the general news column of the *Official Gazette*. The Consultative Committee of the Prime Minister's Office had earlier been aware of the necessity of Government PR in attaining good results for national administrative policy, and had been examining a potential plan for it. They concluded that they should start by opening to the public the documents and materials that each Government organization possessed in order to create better communications between them and the public. As a result there was discussion about the publication of such an organ. However, with the lack of finance, they found that it was too difficult to publish it as an independent publication at that time and concluded that the most practical method was to publish it as a supplement to the *Official Gazette*. In consequence, with the agreement of the Council of Vice-Ministers on 8th June, 1953, they started to put out the *Commentary* (8 pages) as a supplement from 1st July of the same year, issuing it on the first and fifteenth day of every month from then on. After volume 6, they started to charge 5 yen for it and sell it to individual members of the general public who wished to buy.

It is said that the *Commentary* should have really been published separately from the start but they took the step of trying to publish it as a supplement for a while. Later, however, following historical examples of the past it was put out as a separate publication. In May 1957 *PR Information* (published every 10 days) was separated from *Commentary* and was later re-titled *Current Movement: a Window on the Government*. It is interesting to observe how the *Official Gazette* has developed and taken the lead in Government publicity and PR throughout the eras.

NOTES:

1. Printing Bureau, Ministry of Finance, *History of the Printing Bureau of the Ministry of Finance*, Tokyo 1962, p. 464.

2. KONDO, Kanehiro, "Official Gazette and Government PR", *Government Publications Monthly* 6:9, p. 7.

3. Government Publications at Present

GOVERNMENT PUBLICATIONS FROM A STATISTICAL VIEWPOINT

It is said that there are 6,000 items the Government publishes
annually, some say even 9,000. Specific statistics for general
publication are usually vague and inconclusive, this being
especially true in the case of Government publications. It is,
therefore, very difficult to arrive at an accurate number of
items the Government puts out.

In reviewing historical records, it is difficult to compile an
accurate statistical record because of the fact that each era
used different methods in recording information. Before the
war the Statistics Bureau of the Cabinet had established a repu-
tation in regard to gathering, compiling and publishing statistics. After the war, however, the National Diet Library took
over the gathering and compiling, though the Statistics Bureau
still published all of the material. For early Meiji, we do
not have reliable statistics as to how much and what was
published.

Now let us observe the change in quantity of Government publications after the Meiji era. As previously indicated, even though
the Meiji Government did put a lot of effort into publishing,
there is not enough evidence to substantiate exactly how much
was published. The only source we have is the *Copyright Catalogue* in which the number of items published during the period
October 1875 to December 1876 is listed. According to this
source, 365 items are listed as official documents published by
the Government.

From 1876 to 1918 the section in the *Copyright Catalogue* on
Government publications was only sporadically included. However, from 1918 onward this section was included in every issue,
greatly facilitating present day documentation of Government
publications. From these records we know that up until around
1939, of all that was published, Government publications consistently totalled between 30 and 40 per cent. From 1939 on
throughout the war years all publications gradually decreased.
After the war, however, the percentage of Government publications
to all other publications, slowly increased, reaching a peak in
1958 and since then has gradually decreased. The highest percentage that Government publications ever reached was 30 per
cent.

Table 1 indicates the number of items published during the decade 1965 to 1974 and is taken from the *Japan Statistical Yearbook*. The number of government publications published during these 3 years shows a slight increase:

	a. Whole Publications	b. Government Publications	b/a x 100
1965	17,139	3,399	19.8
1966	18,490	3,528	19.1
1967	20,387	4,591	22.5
1968	20,113	4,681	23.3
1969	22,267	4,789	21.5
1970	25,445	2,340	9.2
1971	23,849	1,875	7.9
1972	26,561	2,355	8.9
1973	27,794	2,622	9.4
1974	30,481	3,513	11.5

Table 1.   The Titles of Government Publications for ten years
(Books)
(This is based on the *Japan Statistical Yearbook*)

2,355 items in 1972, 2,622 items in 1973, and 3,513 items in 1974. Government publications during these 3 years consistently remained around 10 per cent due to a proportional increase in non governmental publications as well.

Up to this point we have seen the general changes in the quantity of government publications from the Meiji era up to the present time.   In order to arrive at an accurate number of

annually printed government publications, a comparative study
done by Suzuki between the *Bibliography of Government Publications* (1945-1958) and the *Japanese National Bibliography* is very
useful.[1] The former is said to be the most voluminous and comprehensive compilation of data in the country, while the latter,
though not as comprehensive, is used by the prestigious *Japan
Statistical Yearbook*. According to Suzuki's study, the number
of government publications during the five years from 1953 to
1957 consistently reached from around 9,000 to 9,800 annually.
The figures given in the *Japanese National Bibliography*, though
they include periodicals as well, are not much different from
the figures in Table 1, which are taken from the *Bibliography
of Government Publications*. From these various sources it can
be deduced that out of the total number of publications,
periodicals such as magazines, numbered from 1,000 to 1,200
annually; and published books would be around 8,000 per year.
Out of this total it can be figured that 30 or 40 per cent
consisted of government publications.

As we have seen, government publications are not only numerous,
but also very important sources of information in regard to,
among other things, a better understanding of various aspects
of Japanese social life, politics, economics and education.
The compilation of this statistical data is unequalled as a
source of information.

USE AND GENERAL KNOWLEDGE OF GOVERNMENT PUBLICATIONS FROM A
STATISTICAL VIEWPOINT

Up to now the statistical aspect of publications have been shown.
Later the various types of government publications which are
published will be explained. However at this time, it would be
helpful to view government publications from the user's standpoint.

Generally speaking, government publications are either primarily
historical documents showing the developing process of administration and policy, or general academic documents such as annual
and statistical research reports, which contain current figures
relating to politics, economics and culture. The former is
valuable for historical researchers, and the latter for scholars
or the public for their informational content.

Whatever the reason for using government publications the people
have a right as well as an obligation to understand state policy
better by utilizing the statistics reported therein. In Japan

there has not been much understanding between the Government and the Japanese populace due to the dominant Government attitude that the people do not need to know the reasons for administrative actions. This attitude was designed to make the people rely unquestioningly on the Government and its decisions. It can be understood then how public access to government documents was discouraged. Lately because of a relaxed Government attitude and a growing interest by the public in government publications, the significance and the importance of their availability is being recognized; and as a result government publications are now well used.

It is said that in the United States, government publications are highly used in developing new products. In our country we have not yet reached the stage where this material is effectively being used in product planning, though it is true that some companies have begun using government publications as textbooks in their training classes.

To further understand how government publications are used, let (2) us look at two sources: the *Research on Government Publications* put out by the Prime Minister's Office, and a survey made by the Service Center for Government Publications. The purpose of the Prime Minister's study is to determine how much the public knows about the existence and distribution of government publications, while the purpose of the Service Center's survey was to determine the extent to which government publications are used. The Prime Minister's study is based on urban adult males between the ages of 18 to 59 who live in Japanese cities of more than 100,000 people. It is a unique study in that it shows not only the present utilization of government publications, but also their potential use. Interviews took place in June 1967; 2,262 out of 3,000 men (75.4%) responded to the survey.

According to this survey:

1. Those who recognized what government publications are:

     YES ----- 37%
     NO ------ 63%

The occupations of those who answered YES:

        Administration -------------------------- 68%
        Technical and clerical professions-------- 51%

Students ------------------------------- 48%
Commercial and industrial service
professions --------------------------- 36%
Agricultural, forestry and fishery
professions --------------------------- 25%
Labourers ------------------------------ 22%

2. Those who know what the *Official Gazette* is:

YES ----- 50%
NO ------ 50%

Those who have used government publications before-53%

Occupations:

Administration ------------------- 99%
Technical and clerical
professions ---------------------- 72%
Liberal professions -------------- 68%

Those who know what the *Proceedings of the Diet*
are ---- less than 30%

3. Those who have read government publications
other than the *Official Gazette* ----------- 20%
Those who have seen ----------------------- 10%
Those who have never seen ----------------- 70%

Among those who have read, what they read:

*White Papers -------------- 58%
Periodicals -------------- 39%
Books -------------------- 43%

* The White Paper is well read, probably due to influence
from the news media.

4. Purpose for using government publications:

*For business --------------------------- 53%
For general knowledge ------------------- 28%
For personal study ---------------------- 21%
For understanding the policy of the
government ------------------------------ 9%

For research ------------------------- 9%
For other reasons -------------------- 15%

*This shows that government publications are used for
business purpose quite often.

5.   Those who know their Local Sales Agency for the *Official
      Gazette*, the Service Center for Government Publications
      and the Service Station:

         Local Agency for the Official
         Gazette ------------------------------- 13%
         Service Center for Government
         Publications ------------------------ 9%
         Service Station --------------------- 6%

A total of 28% have some knowledge, while 79% have never
heard these names.

The figures appear to be low, but the number of people actually
using these materials is quite high - especially among the
educated and the intelligensia. It seems that the higher an
individual's level of education and living becomes, the more
he tends to be aware of government publications; and he will
also know how to use them.

The following statistics were compiled from the November 1969
survey conducted by the Service Center for Government Publications. They deal with the occupations of those who use government publications.

         Company and bank employees ----------- 48%
         Government officials ------------------ 23.7%
         Students ------------------------------ 6.7%
         Liberal professions ------------------- 4%
         Non-restricted trades ----------------- 3.2%
         Teachers ------------------------------ 2.4%
         Unemployed and others ----------------- 12%

Half of the users are company and bank employees, while percentage wise government officials are next. A user study done
in August 1963[3] shows similar results, but in the 1969 study the
percentage of company and bank employees rose. As the study
shows a 100 per cent overall increase in people using the
center over a couple of years, it can be expected that in the
future these materials will be more and better used.

NOTES:

1. SUZUKI, Yukihisa, "Collection of Material Source for Research and Government Publications", Proceedings of the 1st Japan-U.S. Conference on Libraries and Information Science in Higher Education, Tokyo, 1970, p. 148.

2. Office of Public Relations, Prime Minister's Secretariat, *A Study of Government Publications*, Tokyo, 1967, p. 172.

3. NAITO, Hidetaka, "The Present Condition of the Center Based on the Results of the Questionnaire", *Government Publications Monthly* 7:11, Tokyo, 1963, p. 8.

CHAPTER 2
DEFINITION OF GOVERNMENT PUBLICATIONS

'Government publications' (Seifu Kankobutsu) is a relatively
new term and its interpretation and usage are not yet widely
understood. The term came into use at the end of World War II
in 1945. At first the term was seldom used, but as the Council
for the Diffusion of Government Publications, established in
1956, started to promote the activities of the Service Center
for Government Publications, the term became more familiar to
the· people.

Government publications were called Official Issue (Kanpan) or
Official Print (Kanpan) in the Meiji era so that the people
could distinguish them from privately printed publications.
From the Taisho and up into the Showa period they were called
Books by the Government (Kancho Kanko Tosho) or Official Publications (Kancho Kankobutsu). After World War II, they were
called Publications by the Government and Municipal Offices
(Kankocho Kankobutsu), Official Publications (Kancho Kankobutsu)
or Government Publications (Seifu Kankobutsu). The long-used
term Official Publications (Kancho Kankobutsu) is still widely
used due to the fact that the general public is well acquainted
with its meaning and purpose. Such changes in terminology all
depended on how various national organizations were generically
named. Since the Meiji era national organizations have been
generally called Government Offices (Kancho). These national
entities of course were also called the "government" (Seifu).
However, the term SEIFU "government" had a narrower perspective
than the term KANCHO "government offices", which indicated the
administrative and national levels of government. After the
war, the term KANCHO KANKOBUTSU "official publications" was
replaced by the term SEIFU KANKOBUTSU "government publications".

There is no clear definition of government publications, as

definitions vary depending upon country and person. An international publication defines the term as follows: "all documents, volumes, periodicals and other works published by order and at the expense of the public authorities of these States". (*UNESCO Bibliographical Handbook* vol. 7). The Institute of Administrative Sciences defines them as follows: "official publications are publications for which public authorities or public law entities are responsible as authors or publishers".

Now let us look at some other definitions from the standpoint of Japanese laws and regulations. First of all, according to "The Ministry of Finance Establishment Law" and the paragraph of the Printing Bureau in the "Official Regulations concerning the Organization of the Ministry of Finance", government publications include the "official gazette, statutes and public relations documents, etc.". (Paragraph 2, Article 16 of the Ministry of Finance Establishment Law) The National Diet Library Law stipulates that government publications are publications put out "by or for any agency of the government". (Paragraph 1, Article 24 of the National Diet Library Law). Also, according to the agreement "Concerning the Reinforcement of the Diffusion of Government Publications" which was approved by the Cabinet on 2nd November, 1956, government publications are "the printed matter compiled by government organizations with the intention of selling or distributing it". In addition to the above, the term is further defined to include reports, survey reports, documents and statistics, etc., which are compiled under the auspices of the various ministries, agencies, public corporations and other government related organizations". The above is an official definition of government publications.

The following is a definition by an individual, Heizo Miyata:

> "Government publications are documents and materials based upon government policy and planned, edited or published by the various organs of the government as a part of their official work. Government publications include not only those exclusively planned, edited and published by the government, but also those which, though published by an outside organization, are planned and edited by the government, and those publications which are planned and edited by an outside organization but published by the government. However, material that is compiled and published by private organizations under government subsidization cannot be considered a government publication, as in this case

the government was in no way responsible for
compilation". (1)

Though the above definitions view government publications from
different perspectives, they are in essence the same. Up to
this point it can be seen how difficult it is to define exactly
what government publications are. First, there is a difficulty
in defining precisely what government organizations are.
Secondly, there is a difficulty in determining the subject
matter of government publications, as each item published tends
to vary greatly as to content.

Now let us examine the Government and its structure. In a
broad, comprehensive sense, Government includes all of the
branches of the legislature, judicature and the administration.
Sometimes it simply means the state. In a narrow sense, it
only means the cabinet and the administrative organs. In Japan
the latter interpretation is often used. When speaking in
terms of government publications, it must be conceded that
Government be defined to include the legislature, judicature
and the administration. If government publications are interpreted to mean only those published by the administrative
branch of the Government, the publications of other branches
would have to be excluded. There should be no distinction, and
it is generally accepted that government publications also
include the publications of the legislative and judicial
branches as well.

There are many opinions about what to include in the scope of
government organizations. In a broad sense they comprise the
Government and all other government-related bodies. In a narrow
sense, they comprise internal subdivisions, external bureaus,
specific authorities and auxiliary organs. But as these government-related organizations are only a substitute agency for the
Government itself, receiving investments or grants from the
Government, it is imperative to broaden the definition of
government organizations. These government-related organizations are also subject to the budget and audit committees of
the Diet.

To summarize, there are two general concepts of government
organizations. One is a broad interpretation and the other is
a narrow one. The broad interpretation includes the organs of
legislation, justice and administration, plus all government-
related organizations. The narrow interpretation excludes
government-related organizations. The broad definition is

generally accepted. For example, at the National Diet Library,
not only are the publications of each ministry and agency of
the legislative, judicial and administrative branches included,
but also those of national universities and public corporations
as well. There is, however, a distinction between national and
local government. When we say the Government, it is taken to
mean the national Government. The element of confusion in the
use of the term is due to the fact that sometimes local bodies
are included in the definition.

There is another problem of definition that should be examined.
Though "publication" means published work, it usually does not
include certain types of documents, such as office paper work
and accounting books.

As will be explained in detail later, there are three types of
government publications: routine official work, commissioned
work and compilations. These publications are either published
by the Government itself or by a commercial company. Due to
these different aspects of character, there are a variety of
government publications. In the broad sense, any work that the
Government had a part in writing, editing, supervising, printing
or publishing can be called a government publication. In the
narrow sense, government publications are works actually done
by the various government organizations; being made, edited and
published by themselves.

It is difficult to define government publications as we have
seen; and it is probably more appropriate to interpret government organizations and publications from a broader perspective.

NOTES:

     1. MIYATA, Heizo, "Government Organizations' Materials
        and Their Use ---Social Sciences", Text for the 3rd
        Documentation Course sponsored by the Ministry of
        Education, Tokyo, 1963, pp. 285-

BIBLIOGRAPHY:

     1. TANABE, Yoshitaro, "Government Organizations'
        Materials and Their Use ---Publications and Cata-
        logues of the Foreign Governments and International
        Organizations", ibid., Tokyo, 1963, pp. 207-238.

2. SAKUMA, Nobuko, "How to Use the Government Organizations' Materials and Bibliography (I)", *Biblos* 21:3, Tokyo, 1970.

3. KUROKI, Tsutomu, "Collecting and Supplying Government Publications", *Library World* 18:2, Kyoto, 1968.

CHAPTER 3
TYPES AND CHARACTERISTICS OF GOVERNMENT
PUBLICATIONS

1.   Types of Government Publications

The diverse material put out by government organizations are the
result of work done in each area of the judicial, legislative
and administrative branches of the Government. As government
publications are published for various purposes, there is a lot
of diversity as to content, and form. In order to classify
government publications, we could apply the same classification
scheme as used for regular commercial publications. For example,
(a) classify them into what we call primary and secondary
materials, depending on whether they are original or derivative;
(b) treat them as monographs or serials, according to their published form; (c) divide them by type into books, pamphlets,
periodicals, and audio visual materials such as tapes and films.

Usually we classify government publications according to their
characteristics, unlike regular commercial materials. In the
United States, A.M. Boyd, an authority in this field, and L.F.
Schmeckebier classify them according to their publishing organization and their subject matter. In Japan, Yoshitaro Tanabe,
Katsuichiro Yamauchi and others are trying to classify according
to purpose and subject matter.

The following is an example of classification for government
publications in the light of the classification of Tanabe and
Yamauchi:

1. Classification according to the purposes of the publication:

        1. Reports of administrative policy, etc., to the
            people.

        2. Reference materials of immediate necessity for each

ministry and agency.

3. Reference and guidance materials for government-related organizations.

4. Academic investigations and research reports on the administration of each ministry and agency.

5. Records and documents as a record for future use.

6. Public relations material.

7. Materials for foreign countries.

2. Classification by subject matter. Materials are usually classified according to content, but in the case of government publications, they are classified either under the legislative, judicial or administrative branch of the Government.

1. Parliamentary materials

   a. Proceedings (minutes of plenary sessions, minutes of committees)

   b. Laws and regulations (laws, cabinet orders, legislative bills)

   c. Treaties (Cabinet council, Cabinet convention, Cabinet consent)

   d. Petition, appear materials

   e. Reference materials for committees, etc.

2. Judiciary materials

   a. Court records (court decisions, judicial precedents)

   b. Judicial investigation documents

   c. Reports on judicial research

3. Administrative materials

   a. Administrative reports (annual reports of the

Administration, official business reports)

b. Investigative reports; the actual conditions and
    situations of the subject of the Administration
    (White paper)

c. Statistical reports (designated statistical
    reports, individual statistical research, business
    statistical reports)

d. Academic study reports (bulletins of research
    institutions, special study reports)

e. Documents of public announcements (right of
    ownership for industry, industrial standards)

f. Records of committees and councils (records of
    investigation and deliberation)

g. Administrative manuals (organization, laws and
    regulations, office work and business)

h. Administrative guidance materials (résumés of
    business practice, explanation, commentary)

i. Materials for educational study and training
    (teaching materials)

j. Public relations materials (PR information, news
    of the day)

k. Records and documents of administrative history
    (material of administrative history, history of
    ministries and agencies)

l. Materials for foreign countries (materials in
    foreign languages for abroad)

m. Secondary materials (bibliographies, catalogues)

These are not generally accepted classification schemes; there
are also other schemes based on different points of view.

2.   Characteristics of Government Publications

Government publications differ from regular publications in the
distinctiveness of the author and subject matter, and the unique
method of publication and distribution. By studying and analysing the author, subject matter and the publishing system, the
special features of government publications may be brought to
light.

From one viewpoint, materials can be divided into two categories: those that are useful for general knowledge and those
that are intended for research and study. As far as government publications are concerned, it is generally acknowledged
that they are used mainly for research and study. The Government is the largest investigative organization and produces a
vast quantity of statistical documents; and these documents
are very basic and essential in order to grasp the entire
perspective of Japanese social life, politics, economics and
education.

In regard to the contents of these materials, they vary from
laws, which are indispensable to social life, and the white
paper, which is an analysis of the result of state policy, to
the practical and educational, e.g. *Weather in Japan, the
Chinese Characters Designated for Daily Use, Current Kana
Orthography and Declensional Kana Endings*. I have checked the
total of published government publications in relation to their
subjects. Although the data is not up-to-date, I believe the
general tendency has not changed much.(1)

According to my investigation, the number of government publications classified by subject in 1955 and 1964 are shown in
Table 2. This classification by subject is based on the N.D.C.
(Japanese Decimal Classification). In 1955 publications relating to the social sciences numbered 2,500, items accounting
for 54.0 per cent of all government publications. These were
followed by industry with the total of 1,269 items or 26.5 per
cent, and engineering with 561 items or 11.7 per cent. Again
in 1964, publications in the social sciences amounted to 44 per
cent, followed by 33 per cent for industry and 11 per cent for
engineering. Obviously the publications in the social sciences
field outnumber the others. It is also characteristic of
government publications that they include a considerable quantity of publications on industry and engineering. Publications
on the social sciences, industry and engineering taken together,
totalled about 90 per cent. When comparing the number of

government publications with the number of regular publications, the field of literature has the highest number followed by the social sciences and engineering. As far as the social sciences and engineering are concerned, we can find a common trend in government publications and regular publications. However, it is more remarkable in government publications.

Judging from this research, the social sciences, industry and engineering, clearly hold a large portion of the field. In other words, as far as quantity is concerned, there are so many publications in these fields that other subjects are unnoticeable by comparison.

Another characteristic of government publications is their type. The following statistical analysis is also based on my research. Table 3 is a list of the number of government publications classified by their type. As mentioned already, this scheme of classification depends upon the individual, and those used here are my own.

According to this, investigative and statistical reports (type e) totalled 26.2 per cent with the highest number of 376, followed by official business reports (type d) with 188 and 13.1 per cent. As we can see from this table, except for the investigative and statistical reports there are no particular distinctions. It must be noted, however, that this statistical analysis is done exclusively on books. Therefore, we cannot apply these figures and percentages directly to all materials because there are many publications put out in the form of pamphlets and magazines, also PR activities have become more active since the war. Nevertheless investigative and statistical materials are definitely government publications, and as a matter of fact, one book in four is in this category.

There are other aspects of government publications. One of these is materials which are secret state documents and are not included in the general run of government publications. Usually they are distinguished from general documents and are called non-departmental documents. Among the non-departmental documents, which are classified information, there are three categories: secret documents either with or without time limits and top secret documents. Another aspect of publication is the difference in distribution between commercial and government publications. Distribution of government publications can be divided three ways; (1) free distribution, (2) prime cost distribution, offering at cost, and (3) sale at market price.

Subjects (N.D.C.)	1955				1964			
	general publications	(%)	government publications	(%)	general publications	(%)	government publications	(%)
0 General works	552	(4.4)	108	(2.2)	352	(2.8)	21	(1.5)
1 Philosophy	775	(6.2)	3	(0.1)	772	(6.3)	3	(0.1)
2 History	842	(6.7)	18	(0.4)	902	(7.3)	71	(4.9)
3 Social sciences	2,697	(21.5)	2,580	(54.0)	2,878	(23.2)	636	(44.4)
4 Natural sciences	1,088	(8.7)	209	(4.4)	1,142	(9.2)	39	(2.7)
5 Engineering	1,188	(9.5)	561	(11.7)	1,693	(13.7)	170	(11.9)
6 Industry	940	(7.5)	1,269	(26.5)	1,105	(8.9)	473	(33.0)
7 Arts	918	(7.3)	29	(0.6)	819	(6.6)	19	(1.3)
8 Linguistics	647	(5.2)	4	(0.1)	508	(4.1)	1	(0.1)
9 Literature	2,882	(23.0)	0		2,223	(17.9)	0	
	12,529	(100.0)	4,781	(100.0)	12,398	(100.0)	1.433	(100.0)

Table 2   The Titles of Publications on Subjects

(general publications is based on the *Japan Statistical Yearbook*.

government publications is based on the *Bibliography of Government Publications* (1955)
and the *Japanese National Bibliography* (1964))

		Titles of publications	(%)
a	Reference materials for administration	141	(9.9)
b	Administrative reports	125	(8.7)
c	Administrative guidance materials	139	(9.7)
d	Official business reports	188	(13.1)
e	Investigative and statistical reports	376	(26.2)
f	Academic study reports	23	(1.6)
g	Records and documents	144	(10.1)
h	Public relations materials	112	(7.8)
i	Materials for foreign countries	36	(2.5)
j	Others	149	(10.4)
	Total	1,433	(100.0)

Table 3   The number of government publications classified by their type. (1964)

The materials that belong to (1) are published by government organizations and are normally not for sale. Some of them are distributed to interested organizations, but the quantity is limited due to budgetary restrictions.

A further aspect is printing. Letterpress printing is very common in commercial publishing. Government publications, however, are not all published in this way due to prohibitive costs and are often published by offset methods, mimeographed, or written by hand. This is also due to the limited number of copies of some publications which are issued. Another reason is that neither the interdepartmental materials nor general materials are as yet generally available to the public.

NOTES:

1. KUROKI, Tsutomu, "Study on Government Publications",
    Annual of the Japan Association of Library Science
    14:2, Tokyo, 1967, pp. 18-22.

BIBLIOGRAPHY:

1. TANABE, Yoshinori, "Government Organizations'
    Materials and Their Use ---the Publications and
    Catalogues of Foreign Governments and International
    Organizations", Text for the 3rd Documentation
    Course sponsored by the Ministry of Education,
    Tokyo, 1963, pp. 207-238.

2. YAMAUCHI, Katsuichiro, "Collecting and Limits of
    the Government Publications of Japan", *Management
    and Use of Magazines*, compiled by the Documentation
    Control Committee of JLA (Japan Library Association),
    Tokyo, 1967.

3.   White Paper

Originally the White Paper meant the official report of the
British Government. It is called the White Paper because of
the colour of its front cover. Likewise an official report
submitted to the British Parliament was called the Blue Book
because of its blue cover.

Many countries have imitated this custom and started to use the
terms "white paper" and "blue book" for official reports of
their own Governments, including Japan. Some people give the
white paper the nickname of a report "in a fish bowl" which
means a report without fear or favour in full view of the people.
It is generally accepted that the term White Paper is the
collective name for all reports which are made upon the basic
facts and the actual situation of state affairs.

With regard to the definition of the white paper, in "Concerning the Control of Government Publications (White Paper, etc.)"
[for reference it is put in Appendix 1] , which is a matter
agreed upon by the Council of Vice-Ministers in 1963, they
define it as follows:

1.   Government publications compiled by the national govern-
     ment organs and agencies. However, the following govern-
     ment publications shall be excluded:

     (a)   Those that are compiled under the name of an
           individual.
     (b)   Non-departmental documents, although those that are
           not for sale but are widely distributed are
           included.
     (c)   Monthly magazines, pamphlets and the like, because
           those which are included should be in book form.

2.   Since the primary object shall be to make the basic facts
     and actual conditions of politics, economics and society
     as well as of the policy of the government known to the
     public, the following shall be excluded: commentaries on
     laws and regulations, statistical research reports and
     materials used only to define the operations of each
     present government office and agency.

Basically the white paper is a report that the Government is
to submit to the Diet. It is also the official report that is
made for the purpose of directly informing the public. It is

generally interpreted that the former is the report that is
published from the original submitted to the Diet by the Government. The latter is the official report in the administrative
annual report that the government puts out in order to describe
the actual and recent conditions of the administration.
Furthermore, the former obliges the Government to report to the
Diet under the provisions of the laws concerned. The latter,
however, is a report submitted voluntarily on the actual state
of their administration.

HISTORY

The first white paper ever to appear in Japan was published by
the Economic Planning Agency (formerly the Economic Stability
Headquarters) in July 1947 under the Katayama Cabinet, its
title being the *Report of the Actual Conditions of the Economy*.
For this paper the Government had gathered as many statistics
and materials as possible. The White Paper was published in
order that people could be made aware of the actual economic
situation and show that by working together with the Government
the economic crisis could be overcome. It was a small booklet
of no more than 30 pages, but it had great public appeal and
created quite a sensation.

In 1948 a report entitled *Fair Trade Commission's Annual Report*,
which was submitted to the Diet by the Fair Trade Commission,
was put out as a result of the act "Concerning Prohibition of
Private Monopoly and Maintenance of Fair Trade" (April 1947).
It was the first appearance of this report which is popularly
known as the *Monopoly White Paper*.

In August 1949, the Ministry of International Trade and Industry
(MITI) announced a report entitled *Concerning the Conditions
of International Trade in Japan*. It was then published and
marketed by the Asahi Newspaper Company under the title *White
Paper on International Trade; Concerning the Actual Conditions
of International Trade in Japan*. It was the first publication
ever to have the term "white paper" in its title.

In 1950 the following two white papers were published; the
first white paper of the Ministry of Labour entitled *Analysis
of Labour Economy for 1949: a Labour Economy under Stability
Planning*, and *Present Conditions of National Land Construction*
by the Ministry of Construction. In the first half of the
1950s, a couple more white papers were published.

In the latter half of the 1950s, as if to emphasise the results of continually improving statistical research data, one white paper after another appeared. By 1960 most of the major ones were in publication. Since then the number of white papers has increased remarkably. However, among what were called white papers by the media there were many that were not even official reports. On 2nd December 1960 *The Fifth White Paper on Health and Welfare* for 1960 was put before the Cabinet Council Meeting. It referred to the following two issues:

1. Without the knowledge of the Cabinet Council and before its official release, some parts of the white paper were published in the newspapers.

2. In what was published there were some parts which could lead to misunderstanding by the public.

Up to this time, the white paper had generally been taking a critical attitude towards the Government with regard to the level of living standards. The controversial white paper for 1960 pointed out that there was an increase in poverty despite the Income-Doubling Program which contributed to the economic growth in the country. It also insisted on the necessity for a social security policy, thereby revealing the weak point of the Government and ruling party. Though it was approved by the Cabinet Council at that time, it was agreed that white papers published by government offices and agencies should henceforth be more carefully treated.

Riding the crest of the boom in white papers, some of questionable quality also appeared. When the white paper of Construction was put out in 1963, Ichiro Kono, the then Minister of Construction, brought up the problem of over-issuing of white papers at the Cabinet Council meeting. This was followed by an agreement "Concerning the Control of Government Publications (White Papers, etc.)", which was made by the Council of Vice-Ministers with the purpose of classifying and controlling white papers. In regard to their content, it was agreed that their purpose should be to make the public fully aware of current conditions of politics, economics and society. As far as the prospects and the perspective of government policy were concerned, except for a matter that was already officially acknowledged, it should be necessary to obtain the consent of the Cabinet Council before publishing important government policy in the white paper. In regard to authorizing the white paper, limits were set as to the number which could officially

have the title of white paper. This control was put into effect
in order to prevent administrative departments from unreasonably
overemphasizing the necessity for future government policy and
also to prevent white papers from being biased. The contribution of this control in allowing each ministry and agency to
reflect on the purpose and responsibility of the varied reports
and papers they put out should also be recognized.

The Cabinet Council turned down the *White Paper on National
Living for 1968* and sent it back to the agency concerned. This
was a rare case and ultimately resulted in public discussion on
white papers. In principle the purpose of government publications, including white papers, is to make the Government's
policy clearly and precisely known to the public. Consequently,
each publication is supposed to be written objectively and
scientifically. This was true especially after the war when it
was made an invariable principle to have the contents of government publications free from bias and prejudiced opinions.

This controversial *White Paper on National Living for 1968* was
written by the Economic Planning Agency and was brought to the
Cabinet Council on 4th July 1967. Each member of the Cabinet
criticized that "in this white paper there are some expressions
and data that could possibly lead to public misunderstanding".
It was, therefore, rejected by the Cabinet. Specifically, it
was criticized because the topic of Development of the Priority
to Life, which was the subtitle of the white paper, was not
clear at all. As to the data, they were dissatisfied with the
index statistics for the environmental standards of life, which
were used in a comparison with other countries concerning
leisure activity. The Economic Planning Agency used the data
in the "Total Holdings of the Public Libraries" and the "Park
Area in Cities per capita" for the index to make an international comparison. These figures were obviously below the
average for other countries, and were a sore point with a
Government which wanted to boast of Japan being number two in
terms of GNP.

The withdrawn white paper was checked and re-examined by the
Economic Planning Agency. They changed the title of "Development of the Priority to Life" to "Development of the Priority
to National Living". Although they did not change the data
used for comparison, they changed the term "leisure" to
"enriched spare time". On 8th July 1969, this *White Paper on
Health and Welfare* was represented and eventually approved by
the Cabinet Council. Thus after much discussion over the

"leisure" issue the Government had to acknowledge the contents
of the white paper, mainly because they feared public opinion.
In the end the contents and statistics in that white paper were
both untouched and officially published. Through their negotiations the Economic Planning Agency tried to impress on the
public that they had resisted political pressure by changing
neither the main content nor the original figures; but that by
merely changing some of the wording they had acknowledged the
authority of the Cabinet. They firmly withstood the idea that
they changed the figures, because this was contrary to the
principle of the white paper. However, this issue has left us
with a feeling of uneasiness because of the fact that the
Government tried to make them change not only some terminology
but also the very contents of the white paper.

OUTLINE

According to definition and history, white papers may be divided
into three categories as follows:

1. Those which are reported to the Cabinet and published after
    its approval.

2. Those which are published and submitted to the Diet under
    the provisions of the law.

3. Reports and other papers which are not officially named
    "white papers".

In regard to (1) and (2) according to the list annexed to the
report of "Concerning the Control of Government Publications
(White Papers, etc.)", there were 25 kinds of this type of white
paper as of the end of 1969.

1. Those reported to the Cabinet and published after their
    approval.
    (Concerned Agency/Name of the White Paper)

Prime Minister's Office   - *White Paper on Youth* (Present situa-
                                 tion of Youth Problems and Counter-
                                 measures)

                               - *White Paper on Atomic Energy*
                                 (Annual Report on Atomic Energy)

Economic Planning Agency   - *White Paper on the Economy* (Annual

Report on the Economy)

- *White Paper on National Living*

- *White Paper on World Economics* (Annual Report on World Economics)

Science and Technology Agency
- *White Paper on Science and Technology*

Ministry of Justice
- *White Paper on Crime*

Ministry of Foreign Affairs
- *Blue Book on Diplomacy* (Recent situation)

Ministry of Health and Welfare
- *White Paper on Health and Welfare* (Annual Report of the Health and Welfare Administration)

Ministry of International Trade and Industry
- *White Paper on International Trade*

Ministry of Transport
- *White Paper on Transport* (Annual Report of Transport Economics)

- *White Paper on Marine Transport* (Current Conditions of Marine Transport in Japan)

- *White Paper on Maritime Safety* (Current Conditions of Maritime Safety)

Ministry of Labour
- *White Paper on Labour* (Analysis of Labour Economics)

Ministry of Construction
- *White Paper on Construction* (Present Situation of Land Construction)

Ministry of Home Affairs
- *White Paper on Fire Defence* (Actual Circumstances of Fire and the Present Conditions of Fire Fighting)

2. Those published from a report submitted to the Diet.

Prime Minister's Office   - *White Paper on Monopoly* (Annual
                              Report of the Fair Trade Commission)

                            - *White Paper on Tourism* (Annual
                              Report concerning the Situation of
                              Tourism and the policy to be
                              followed in the coming year)

Ministry of Agriculture   - *White Paper on Agriculture* (Annual
  and Forestry   Report concerning trends in Agri-
                              culture and the policy to be
                              followed in the coming year)

                            - *White Paper on Fishing* (Annual
                              Report concerning Trends in Coastal
                              Fishing and the policy to be
                              followed in coastal fishing and
                              other areas for the coming year)

                            - *White Paper on Forestry* (Annual
                              Report concerning trends in
                              Forestry and the policy for the
                              coming year)

Ministry of International   - *White Paper on Small and Medium
  Trade and Industry   Enterprises* (Annual Report concern-
                              ing trends in such enterprises and
                              the policy for the coming year)

Ministry of Home Affairs   - *White Paper on Local Finance* (Condi-
                              tions of Local Finance)

Each Ministry concerned   - *White Paper on Public Pollution*
                              (Annual Report concerning the condi-
                              tions of Public Pollution and the
                              Preventive Measures for the coming
                              year)

The titles in parenthesis are those used when they are submitted
to the Cabinet Council, including subtitles if any.

There have been various changes in white papers; some which used
to be published annually have been discontinued and some new ones
have been introduced. Examples of discontinued publications

include, the *White Paper on State Property of the Ministry of Finance* which was founded in 1957 and ceased publication in 1963, and the *White Paper on Aviation* (Current Conditions of Civil Aviation) of the Ministry of Transport, founded in 1957, which was also discontinued in 1963, being superseded by the *White Paper on Transport*. A further example is the *White Paper on National Income* of the Economic Planning Agency, which was started in 1958 and ceased publication after 9 volumes. It is still published as the *Annual Bulletin of National Income Statistics*, but this is not an official white paper.

In regard to category (3), most other government publications (reports, papers and others) can be included. The following five reports and papers are included in this category and are commonly called white papers. They started from the time of the "Control of White Papers". In addition to these, however, one can also include brief and informal white papers such as the Illustrated White Papers which are not listed here.

Ministry of Health and Welfare	– *Present Conditions of National Diet* (White Paper on National Nutrition)
Ministry of International Trade and Industry	– *Present Conditions of the Electrical Industry* (White Paper on Electric Power)
	– *Industrial Location in Japan* (White Paper on Industrial Location)
	– *Present Situation and Problems of Economic Cooperation* (White Paper on Japan's Economic Cooperation)
Ministry of Labour	– *Actual Conditions of Women's Labour* (White Paper on Women's Labour)

Each of the above is explained in detail in the Part IV, Annotations. In general, these white papers are increasing in quality and quantity each year. This is due to an ever diversifying and expanding administrative system, comprehensive statistical research and the growing interest of people in white papers. The total number of pages in 25 official white papers amounts to roughly 10,000 annually.

Although it is difficult to classify white papers, as each of
them has its own characteristics, they could be divided into
two types, according to the manner of editing. One could then
apply the categories (1) and (2), seen earlier, to these two
types. The first type which corresponds to category (1) includes the annual report, which is edited mainly to analyse the
present situation of each administrative organ. Included in
this type are three subdivisions: those which are analysed
from the same point of view as the previous year, those analysed
from different points of view and those which are analysed
according to specific themes, such as the *White Paper on Education*. The second type which corresponds to category (2) are
the annual reports, which are edited by focusing on an analysis
of the particular direction and trend of each administration's
policy.

The method of compiling and editing white papers will now be
looked at, albeit briefly. Each ministry and agency concerned
has its own schedule fixed every year and it is naturally
related to the proposed publication date for their white paper.
This schedule includes the purpose, policy, procedure and a
plan of execution. Usually the division which manages the
editing of the white paper is in charge of planning the schedule.
As a general rule the schedule will vary little from year to
year, but changes do occur. Once it has been determined an
editorial meeting is held. At this meeting editing policy is
decided. They formulate policy in regard to the contents, but
at the same time, the editing organization and structure are
also considered. It is desirable that they should organize the
project team because government departments are vertical in
terms of control and operation and consequently suffer difficulty
in communicating with one another. It is, therefore, no easy
task to organize the inter-divisional or inter-departmental
project teams and measures must be taken as and when the occasion
demands. In other words, the staff of each division and department are in charge of their part of the subject matter, but as
it becomes necessary staff from other divisions and departments
are called upon to join in. The job includes gathering the
necessary data in their particular subject fields on the basis
of editorial policy, when the annually aggregated data of
statistical research is announced.

The next step is to prepare a draft of the white paper on the
basis of the data gathered. When the manuscript is completed
the division which is in charge of the white paper and previously
planned the schedule sets about printing it. The parties

concerned from each department and bureau then check and discuss
this printed copy. As a result of this discussion, the copy
may be corrected and amended. After repeating this process
several times, a final draft is agreed. Meanwhile, in order to
be accurate and thorough the printed copy is discussed with
other interested ministries and agencies. Finally, when the
manuscript has passed the Council of the Ministry or Agency,
it is ready to be printed and bound as a white-covered book.
After this white-covered book has been approved by the Council
of Vice-Ministers and by the Cabinet Council it is ready to be
published. It is then distributed to each government organization. As a rule, it is not allowed to print and publish the
book at this time. White Papers on sale to the public do in
fact rarely have white covers. The Printing Bureau of the
Ministry of Finance prints and publishes most of the white
papers and in addition publishes summaries of them in the
Official Gazette. Commercial newspapers also give good coverage
to their contents. Moreover the Printing Bureau compiles and
publishes the *Summary of White Papers*, which was begun in 1968.
It is compiled in order to take a general view of all the white
papers that were published in the previous fiscal year, adding
some model charts to the comments in the Commentary of the
Official Gazette.

BIBLIOGRAPHY:

1. Printing Bureau, Ministry of Finance, *Story of
    White Paper*, Tokyo, 1970, 62 p.

2. Printing Bureau, Ministry of Finance, *Summary of
    White Papers*, Tokyo, 1969, 450 p.

3. Council of the Diffusion of Government Publications,
    *Catalogue for the Exhibition of the History of
    White Papers*, Tokyo, 1970, 30 p.

CHAPTER 4
PRODUCTION PROCEDURE AND AUTHORSHIP OF
GOVERNMENT PUBLICATIONS

1.   Production Procedure of Government Publications

The Government provides enormous amounts of information through
every possible medium. Supplying information based on an
obligation to report is the very function of government public
relations activities[1]. The quantity of information that the
Government sends out through media such as newspapers, radio,
television and publications, outweighs that produced by any
other source of information. Take the newspapers for example,
information from the Government is their largest news source.
On the other hand, from the Government's point of view the newspaper is a very important medium in order to supply and convey
necessary information to the public.

It would, however, be wrong to say that all government produced
information is recorded or that all the recorded information
is important. Much information is certainly still left un-
recorded. There may be more confidential and secret information
that is not open to the public, on grounds that it would be
against the public interest, than that which is published and
supposedly benefits the public. There is also quite a lot of
information which should be published but is not because the
organization concerned assumed that such information need not
be reported.

In respect to government organizations which are the main
producers of information, the source of information is supposed
to be each division or in some cases, an even smaller group.
This is the case although the information is announced as the
ministry's or agency's. As of 1969 there were a total of
1,025 divisions within the organizations of the Government.
Of course not all of these divisions are producing the same
type or kind of information. The number of topics they cover

is estimated to be nearly 6,000.

Now concerning the production procedure, there are the following two types of information; (1) "designed" information, which is intentionally made, and (2) "non-designed" information, which is spontaneously generated. Both of these types eventually become concrete materials, most of them being in published form. Information from government organizations goes through various production processes.

According to Rokuro Shiina[2] there are three steps:

A.   "The first production" (Scattered information).
         The information here is produced spontaneously as the
         planned work is being done. It lies scattered through-
         out the unit and can, therefore, be called scattered
         information.

B.   "The second production" (Accumulated information).
         The scattered information is a bundle of information
         produced as a result of a business transaction. This
         is the step in which all the scattered information is
         accumulated into each subject group. Some accumulated
         information is stored as "classified information", while
         some is kept within the department, because it is not
         considered valuable for external use. In any event, at
         this stage it is called accumulated information.

C.   "The third production" (Summarized information).
         The accumulated information is summarized at this stage,
         so that it can be offered to the outside world in pub-
         lished form.

Although this lucid and intelligible three step procedure can
explain the production process of all kinds of information, it
is best used as regards business reports and the like which
are produced in such enormous quantities.

We can find various examples of processes in the field of
government publications. Sometimes the first and second stages
are already established at the time of planning, so that the
material can go directly to "the third production". A typical
example of this is designated statistics, which will be
explained in detail later. In this case, the information is
produced and published in accordance with the regulations of
each organization.

Now let us classify these various cases:

1.   Required by law. The compilation or publication is
         compulsory.

2.   Requested by the public. A submission or report is
         necessary, even though not required by any regulations
         such as the Office Duty Regulations of each
         organization.

3.   Information reproduced from the original sources, for
         instance the general public relations documents pro-
         duced by the Public Relations Division of each
         organization.

4.   Information made by entrusted specialists, such as the
         reports of the committees.

5.   The results of surveys or discussions such as the
         records of meetings and academic research papers.

         There are probably many other cases besides these five.

As is well known, government publications are regarded as
associate publications, or the works of a corporate author.
Most other publications are produced by individual authors and
in this case everything in the publication from content to
expression belongs to one single author. Recently, there are
indications that publications by joint authors are on the increase but even in such cases each individual author's accomp-
lishment, achievement and position are recognized.

One of the traits of government publications is that they follow
a different process of production from other publications. As
we have already seen in the process of compiling white papers,
corporate publications involve many people in planning, compiling, editing and publishing. The number of people involved
and the procedure followed for each publication varies, but in
general a group of several people from the section concerned,
or in some cases the whole division, work on producing the
information. They collect data produced by other interested
parties, departments, bureaus and even other related ministries
and agencies and examine it. Once all the data has been
gathered and compiled, the section heads check the draft, amend
and correct it. The manuscript is then ready. Some manuscripts
have to pass the Bureau council or other councils before they

are ready to be published.

NOTES:

1. IDE, Yoshio, *Introduction to Administrative Public Relations*, Tokyo, Keisho Shobo, 1967, p. 32.

2. SHIINA, Rokuro, "A Study on Information Management of Various Organizations in Japan", *Biblos* 14:4, Tokyo, 1963, p. 4.

BIBLIOGRAPHY:

1. KABASHIMA, Tadao, *Creation of Information*, Tokyo, Sanseido, 1969, 261 pp.

2. Editorial Committee of the Information Management Practice Seminar, *Collecting and Materializing Information*, Tokyo, Nikkan Kogyo Newspaper Company, 1965, 237 p.

2.   Public Relations of Government Organizations

OUTLINE

Government Public Relations now seems to be fairly well settled into the administrative system. Apparently, public relations was brought into our country after World War II, though the term "PR" was introduced before World War II when some public relations information activity did exist. As is common knowledge, during the war the Intelligence Bureau was in charge of the governmental job of giving out information to the general public and of controlling propaganda, and frequently they made false information reports. After the war, under the Occupation Forces, as a part of the process of democratization, public relations made a spectacular appearance and was taken into the administration of the Japanese Government. The concept of a modern nation was based on democratic government. As democracy is called the "circulating process of consent", it is a political system that maintains mutual communication between the Government and the public. In this sense, as a representative organization of the Government, the public relations organization has the responsibility of performing tasks relating to the public. That is also the reason why it is believed that public relations plays a leading role in the very existence of the

administration. Therefore, giving accurate information on the
ideas and policies of the Government, putting together the
information and gauging the reaction and opinion of the public
is the business of public relations. Accordingly, with the
continual activity that the administration sustains, it is
obvious that public relations in government organizations will
and must develop.

However, the development of public relations in our country has
not been very smooth. The factors that delayed its development
are as follows: (1) the public's lack of faith in the public
relations of the Government, because under the old system the
reports they made had always been controlled and at times they
were deceptive and incomplete, (2) after the Peace Treaty, with
the strong pressure of the Occupation Forces gone and while in
the course of reorganizing the whole system, public relations
was a newcomer in the administration, and therefore found it
very difficult to maintain its position in the system. Nevertheless, owing to the efforts made in rearranging the system and
strengthening the foundation of public relations, its position
was finally established.

Now let us look at the present mechanism of public relations in
the government. Public relations within government can be
divided in two schemes: one is the public relations unit in
each ministry and agency and the other is the Central Public
Relations Organization. As for the former, each independent
public relations office or division is placed in such ministries
and agencies as follows: the Ministry of Foreign Affairs, the
Ministry of Home Affairs, the Ministry of International Trade
and Industry, the Defense Agency, the National Tax Administration Agency and the Supreme Court. With regard to the rest of
the organizations of the Government, they set up a subdivision
or section of public relations either in the General Affairs
Division or in the Secretarial Division of the Minister's
Secretariat and the Director-General's Secretariat. For the
latter, the Office of Public Relations, in the Prime Minister's
Secretariat of the Prime Minister's Office, has since 1st July,
1960 been responsible.

However, the conditions and systems of each division in charge
of public relations in the individual ministry and agency or
those of the Central Public Relations Organization are varied
due to their own situations and, as has been seen, the
reorganization of the whole system after the war. As a result
of just that, administrative organizations as well as other

organizations in Japan are vertically controlled, and because
the history of public relations is rather short, the present
position and situation of public relations is neither agreeable
nor desirable. Vertically-controlled structure is a typical
tradition in an organization in Japan and, among other things,
it limits the giving and receiving of as much information as
possible from one to another. Supported by the demands of the
times, however, publications relations has been steadily
progressing. The budget sum of the public relations divisions
in recent years can validate this, for example, including both
General Account and Special Account, the budget for government
public relations and other related areas for 1971, amounted to
¥ 7,011,000,000 Japanese yen. Of that amount the Prime
Minister's Office, the Central Public Relations Organization,
was allotted 2,498,000,000 yen and the Ministry of Foreign
Affairs 1,263,000,000 yen. We can substantiate the increase by
comparing the aforementioned budget with that of 1961, which
allotted only 370,000,000 yen to the Prime Minister's Office
and 55,000,000 yen to the Ministry of Foreign Affairs.

PUBLIC RELATIONS MECHANISM IN THE MINISTRY AND AGENCY

Let us observe the structure of the public relations organization in each ministry and agency. Here we will observe specifically what kind of steps are taken to convey information to the
public, rather than to view the entire process of public
relations. Public relations can be classified into two categories, general public relations and individual public relations.
The former relates to information on the administration of the
ministry and agency in general, but also included are many
matters pertaining to their policies. The latter particularly
deals with information related to special subjects that each
bureau or division is in charge of.

The public relations division or section usually performs the
general public relations activities at each ministry and agency.
Individual public relations is, however, mainly performed by
the division and section that are in charge of the special
subject concerned within their own ministry and agency. The
information of the PR division in each ministry and agency is
related to their own PR plan. Ideally this PR plan should keep
pace with the administrative plan made by each division that is
in charge of a special subject. Nevertheless in reality it is
very hard to do so. In regard to general public relations, if
it is executed as mentioned above, it should obtain satisfying
results. The public relations division is assigned the role of

controlling and adjusting both individual public relations and general public relations and of coordinating both. Control and coordination between individual and general PR is needed because the former has innate characteristics which lead to inconsistency, as the complexity and diversity of the administration advance, while the purpose of the latter is to harmonize the whole of public relations within the ministry. Concerning the coordination of individual PR alone, there should not be any great problem as to uniformity and duplication of contents. The PR division is expected to promote a consistency of PR activity, evaluating the independence of each item of individual public relations information that is made by the divisions in charge of the special subjects, and establishing a better contact and cooperation with these divisions.

As has been seen, the PR activity in each ministry and agency has a dual setup, the general public relations of the PR division and the individual PR of the divisions in charge of special subjects. The way PR information is relayed to the public will now be looked at. Firstly, most general and individual PR information is released to the Press Club through the Public Relations Office, which is a PR division in each ministry and agency, taking the form of a "news release" or "press conference". Then the news reporters and TV/radio reporters convey it as the news of the Government to the general public. That is called the indirect method. In this case, the public relations division first discusses with the Public Relations Liaison Committee or the people in charge of PR from the divisions of the special subject the information they are going to release. After they investigate its importance and urgency for public relations, they decide the date and the means of releasing. At this time, the chief or the director of the bureau, department or division explains it in detail in the presence of the Public Relations Office staff. In regard to the press conference, except for emergencies, they keep in contact with the press by holding a regular conference involving directors of the bureaus in each ministry and agency.

On the other hand, as a direct method of public relations activities by the Government, which does not depend on news reporters and others, the Government utilizes commercial newspapers and broadcasting. They put articles and advertisements in the newspapers and magazines under the name of the Office of Public Relations. They also have some regular programs that they sponsor and put some advertisements on television and radio. Among these means, sponsoring a program has appeared rather

recently. Although it is planned and executed by the Government, it seems, in a way, that it can also be classified as an
indirect method, for they use commercial newspapers and private
broadcasting.

Both the PR division and the divisions in charge of special
subjects also deliver information to the general public by means
of such media as printed matter, audiovisual materials and PR
automobiles. This is not, however, always done exclusively by
the Government. Sometimes the Government uses their local
agency or other government related organization in order to
better and more efficiently publicize, and sometimes they take
a different route such as going through the PR division of the
local governments or some other organizations. Governmental
PR information, therefore, reaches the public through many
channels. In so far as the job of the PR division in the ministry and agency is concerned, as soon as the operational (or
special subject) divisions have produced their own printed
materials or audiovisual materials and are ready to publish
them, the PR division, as the gatekeeper and controller of PR
information in the ministry and agency, is supposed to print
and publish a summary of the contents, which the operational
divisions put out. Actually, however, the public relations
divisions in the Japanese administrative organization are not
playing a perfect role of supervisor and controller of public
relations. Take printed matter, for instance, most of the many
PR publications are planned and published by the operational
divisions in charge of special subjects on their own. Some of
them are immediately disclosed to the public and the organizations concerned, without even being checked by the PR division's
supervisor in their own ministry. At best after these publications are put out the PR division may be able to make a rather
intensive investigation of them and check them out.

In observing the structure and organization of public relations
in the ministry and agency, we cannot overlook the cooperation
between public relations of the national government and that of
the local governments. As Yoshinori Ide[1] points out, the public
relations structure of the national government is set up so that
it can be conveyed and linked to the local government's, and
the local government's public relations can then take over. In
other words, as the public relations organs in each ministry
and agency are connected to the local bureaus and departments
concerned, public relations material is conveyed down to the
metropolis and districts, that is, to the urban and rural
prefectures, then to the cities, towns and villages where

finally it reaches the public. Therefore, almost without fail
the PR division of each ministry and agency plans its program
with due consideration to linking it to the PR activities of
the local entities. Nevertheless the local governments have
their own plan of PR as well. Some local governments do not
have a particularly strong relationship with the national
government and they are not necessarily responsible for sub-
stituting the PR activities of the national government for them.
Accordingly, as far as the PR information at the local government level is concerned, it is up to the local government as to
what to tell the public. In regard to the process of conveying
information from the PR division of each ministry and agency to
the local governments, it is hard to generalize on the subject.
The connection between the PR divisions of the ministry and
agency and those of the local governments is nothing like the
connection between the Central Public Relations Organization
and the PR organs in the local governments, which will be
explained in detail in the next sub-chapter. As for the former,
the public relations divisions of the ministry and agency are
not necessarily more strongly linked to the public relations
organs but rather to the bureaus, departments or other organizations concerned in the local governments. For example, the
Ministry of Education is no less involved with the Committee of
Education in the local governments than with the public relations
divisions there.

Up to this point we have observed the process of public relations
from the provider's standpoint. Viewing it from the receiver's
standpoint, we can find two kinds of processes as follows:

1.   The general public receives PR information of the Govern-
      ment through the divisions concerned in the local
      governments.

2.   The general public receives it through media such as
      printed matter, broadcasting and films that the ministries
      and agencies themselves send out.

CENTRAL PUBLIC RELATIONS ORGANIZATION

As mentioned before, there is the Office of Public Relations in
the Prime Minister's Office which has been the Central Public
Relations Organization for the Government in Japan since 1960.
They are responsible for planning and executing the public
relations aspect of the Government's policy. They not only
offer the information, as when informing the public of the

national goal and policy, but also anticipate the public's
feelings and opinion toward the Government. As regards offering
information, they perform the publicity work by employing
broadcasting, printed matter and audiovisual materials. For
intelligence activity, they assimilate the public's feelings
and reactions by means of public hearings, monitors and surveys
of public opinion.

Thus the Office of Public Relations is supposedly the main organ
of governmental public relations. Actually, however, it is not
that well equipped to carry out this job. In the past, the idea
of reforming and strengthening this Central Public Relations
Organization has often arisen. Certain people are, however,
afraid of the reinforcement of the Central Public Relations
Organization because they believe it would immediately lead to
the loss of freedom of speech and political propaganda. These
are some of the grounds that deter centralization.

Now we will observe the process of public relations at the Office
of Public Relations in the Prime Minister's Office. First of
all, they deal with general public relations, which we have
seen in the previous sub-chapter, i.e. that which covers the
whole governmental system. As we know, the other, individual
public relations, is taken care of by the public relations
division of each ministry and agency. The Office of Public
Relations is obliged to form its own program following the PR
program of the ministries and agencies that are the administrative authorities of the Government. They utilize various kinds
of PR media in order to convey and diffuse information on the
work of the Government. They hold a meeting in respect of the
subject of their PR so that they can discuss and check with
each ministry and agency the appropriate theme and have better
communication between the organizations. They then fix the
theme on the basis of "Very Important for the Government",
"the subject concerned with a number of ministries" and the
"PR activity that needs cooperation and collaboration from
several ministries and agencies". In any case each ministry
and agency is responsible for the content of the PR information
concerned. As the Office of Public Relations gets far larger
a quantity of PR than it can handle by itself, unlike the public
relations division in each ministry and agency which oversees
and supervises the information of their PR, they have to leave
a large part of the PR activities to each ministry and agency.
Relating to this, in respect of the difference of structure
when compared to that of ministries and agencies, the Office
of Public Relations established the Cabinet Press Room in place

of the public relations division in other ministries and
agencies, that deals with the press, serving as a Press Club
for reporters and functioning as a communication window. In
regard to publications, the Office of Public Relations insti-
tuted the Council for the Diffusion of Government Publications,
which serves to promote the good use of these publications,
collecting reports from each ministry and organization on the
dissemination and distribution of government publications, and
undertaking a survey and compiling a catalogue.

Connections between the Office of Public Relations and the
public relations sections of the local entities are stronger
than those between the Office of Public Relations and the
ministry and agency. The Office of Public Relations gathers
the PR programs of the ministry and agency, and compiles them
into the *Public Relations Sources*, monthly, to distribute to
each local government. Ultimately, the local governments
include the PR information of the national government in their
own PR, thus, it is incorporated with that of the Office of
Public Relations which reaches the public through various media.
That is how the PR of the national government relates to that
of the local governments. Consequently, the Office of Public
Relations has an estimate for the local commission in their own
budget, which is allotted each year through the Archives and
Public Relations Division of the Ministry of Home Affairs.

PUBLICITY MEDIA AND GOVERNMENT PUBLICATIONS

Government PR utilizes as much of the media as the commercial
PR publicity does. It makes full use of media such as newspapers, radio, television, magazines, slides and films. The
staff engaged in PR work and the PR researchers conduct
researches on these media, studying which medium would best suit
certain subjects of PR and which media would be most effective.
Some time ago the radio made its influence felt as a medium of
information publicity. Among the broadcasting media, television
is in the limelight at present and the Government is very
enthusiastically coming to grips with this. Nevertheless, the
publication, the long standing medium, has been playing the
leading role for generations and is still the principal publicity medium.

Let us look at current conditions and realities of media utilization in the Office of Public Relations of the Prime Minister's
Office, which are in the forefront of the publication of government PR. They publish some PR magazines such as the commentary

magazine *Current Movement; A Window of the Government,* the
graphic magazine *Photo* and the *Commentary,* the supplement to the
Official Gazette. The first two are distributed free to municipalities, cities, towns and villages, schools, libraries and
other various groups amounting to 40,000 copies each. Secondly,
they sponsor two radio programs and four television programs,
making altogether six regular broadcasting programs - which are
"Miss Fuyuko Kamisaka's Japan Report" and "The Microphone of
Living" on radio, and "The Square of Japan", "Sunday Circle",
"Southern Islands, Northern Islands" and "Reporting Memo of A
Housewife" on TV. They also use wire relay broadcasting. For
audiovisual materials they produce, among other things, slides
and PR films. Thus they make approaches directly to the general
public through a variety of media.

Although aware of its effectiveness for PR, because broadcasting
is quite costly, they are restricted by the budget, and are
sometimes forced to use other media. However, despite the fact
that use of broadcasting will undoubtedly increase in the future,
the printing media, including mass media such as commercial
newspapers and magazines, are still considered to be superior
in many ways and to be the most effective means not only in
Japan but in the whole world.

Any government publication can be considered as PR material,
ranging from leaflets and pamphlets to periodicals or monographs,
which may be quite bulky in volume and are compiled by government organizations. Since the idea of PR is not fully understood nor has it been very well encouraged in Japan, people
tend to consider only official magazines and pamphlets the PR
publications of the Government. Nevertheless, the most fundamental medium for PR is said to be the staff in the government
organizations and the general public who come into contact with
them. The publications mentioned earlier are of course also
important and are based upon reporting work such as business
and production reports, findings, statistical data and the
reports of experts.

Now from the PR standpoint, we can classify these publications
into two categories as follows: one is regular government
publications, for example, proceedings, business reports,
statistical reports and annual reports; and the other is periodicals and monographs on policy and measures of the Government
compiled for the purpose of PR in a narrow sense. Let us
observe the latter a little further. They are usually called
PR magazines. The PR magazines that are compiled by the public

relations divisions vary in subject, form and format. A few of the titles of such periodicals are, *Official Bulletin* (Koho), *Publicity Information* (Koho), *Public Relations Information* (Koho), *Monthly Bulletin* (Geppo) and *Review* (Jiho). The PR magazines published by the ministry and agency can be subdivided into the following three categories.

The first category includes magazines such as *Official Bulletin of the Ministry of International Trade and Industry* by the Ministry of International Trade and Industry, *Official Bulletin of the Ministry of Transport* by the Ministry of Transport and *Food Information* by the Food Agency. Their subject matter is limited to statutes and notices, announcements and the like which deal in part with the announcement of formally decided statutes.

The second category includes magazines that have the title of PR (Information) as follows: *PR Information on Education* by the Ministry of Education and *PR Information on Agriculture and Forestry* by the Ministry of Agriculture and Forestry. The subject matter is limited to summaries and explanations of policy, correspondence, communication and news articles.

The magazines that belong to the third category are, for example, *Health and Welfare* by the Ministry of Health and Welfare and *Transport* by the Ministry of Transport. They also include magazines containing individual PR on each division and office other than the public relations divisions. The subject matter concentrates more on leading articles, trend analysis and commentaries than the second category. Some titles are published by private organizations employing the editorial supervision system which exhibits a combination of PR and communication work.

NOTES:

1. IDE, Yoshinori, *Introduction to Administrative PR*, Tokyo, Keiso Shobo, 1967, p. 81.

BIBLIOGRAPHY:

1. *ibid.*, 301 p.

2. MATSUMOTO, Yoshiharu, "The PR Age and Government Publications; Public Relations, Publicity Information and Official Bulletin", *Monthly Catalog*

of Government Publications 6:4, Tokyo, 1964,
pp. 4-7.

3. KOYAMA, Eizo, *Common Sense for Public Relations*,
Ministry of Education, Tokyo, 1957, 233 p.

4. Office of Public Relations, Prime Minister's Office,
Outline of Our Work, Tokyo, 1960, 23 p.

3.   Government Statistics

STATISTICAL RESEARCH AND GOVERNMENT OFFICES' STATISTICS

In today's society not only in the administrative organizations
but also in universities, research institutes, the press and
even private companies, statistical research and surveys are
conducted as a matter of necessity and the public are making
full use of them. In our daily life we encounter so many statistics through the mass media, such as television and newspapers,
that we can hardly pass a day without meeting statistics.

The ultimate purpose of statistical research is to bring aware-
ness. However, all social phenomena cannot be shown in figures
by means of statistics such as those in statistical researches.
Therefore, statistical research should be considered as a
process in which one attempts to isolate the quantitative side
of social phenomena and eventually obtain statistical data, in
order to analyse and understand these social phenomena more
fully.

It is said that statistical research is a product of capitalist
society. This does not, however, mean that there was no
statistical research in the Middle Ages or in ancient times;
but it means that it has begun to be carried out on a systematic
basis. In a capitalist society, statistical research is carried
out and utilized from all angles and in many fields. For
instance, the capitalist would conduct a piece of statistical
research and utilize it from his viewpoint and ground and so
would the Government. On the other hand the social science
researcher would conduct it from his own standpoint for the
purpose of his own study.

For the most part statistical data has derived from work done by
government offices. Even now in any country, the principal
conductors of statistical research are national and local

governments. In other words, the Government is the biggest
statistics producer, and government statistics play an important
role in the overall production of statistical data. It was not
too long ago that the nation established professional organizations and started statistical research. In the early 19th
century the Statistics Bureau had been founded in developed
countries. Until then statistical data had been dependent on
investigations done by the temples, shrines and churches and
private bodies. Driven by the needs of the administration and
especially the necessity of planning state policy and measures,
and of studying and examining the progress of policy, the nation
itself had to conduct the necessary statistical research.
Accordingly, the nation has come to take over most of the statistical research.

We call the statistical research done by the administrative
organizations of our country the Government (Offices') Statistics
(Kancho Tokei). As regards the specific characteristics of
government statistics, firstly it is designed to be able to
conduct systematic statistical research by virtue of the statistical system based on the Statistics Law. In a way, the subject
of statistics research extends over a wide area such as the
whole country or the urban and rural prefectures. The statistical organizations of the Government, either in a national or
in a local sense, are very well organized, in order that the
statistical researches will be systematically carried out and
operated.

Secondly, they have enough budgetary support to be able to
afford to conduct long-scale statistical research. For example,
it would cost 1,500,000,000 to 2,000,000,000 yen to take a
nation-wide census. Such a large cost would exceed the capa-
bilities of a private organization. Without a sufficient
budget we cannot expect good statistical research and in this
regard government statistics satisfy the requirement.

Thirdly, the Government can by compulsion impose a duty upon
the individual and the corporation who are being investigated
to reply. This is because, in the matter of statistical
research, if the person being investigated should not give a
reply, the planning and execution of the research would be in
vain. They are, however, under an obligation to report only
to the national and local governments. The advantage of legal
force, above all, puts the government statistics in a better
light.

Fourthly, the secondary statistics furnish the government statistics with a large amount of unique data. Secondary statistics are also called indirect statistics research and are based upon the papers and daily records which are made without the purpose of statistical researching. At the ministry and agency of both national and local governments, secondary statistics are being energetically produced. However, not all of them are obliged to be published, though some of them are of more significance than "primary statistics".

Fifthly, they are successfully making efforts to ensure that it is possible to compare their findings with those of other countries. In this modern society, because we have to utilize statistics research most effectively, people are likely to find statistical research without international comparison meaningless. The statistics classification has been prepared working in relation with the International Statistics Association and the Statistics Organization of the United Nations.

Sixthly, though government statistics are conservative, they possess continuity. It may depend on the field and nature of the statistics research, but basically they make it a condition that the important statistics are to be continuous.

Finally, these statistical researches are conducted because they are necessary for the administration. In other words, they do not conduct any statistics research they do not need.

As we have seen, the Government carrying out statistical research is seemingly a good thing in every way. On the other hand, the characteristics seen above stress the marked tendency of statistics research towards officialdom and, without a reform, to become separated from reality, because continuity is overemphasized. It is true that efforts have been made to perfect the system as much as possible by encouraging the developing technology of statistics research, though there may still be some problems of accuracy and reliability in the Government statistics.

STATISTICAL SYSTEM OF OUR COUNTRY

History

The Japanese statistical system started in the fourth year of the Meiji era (1871) when they established the Statistics

Department in the Ministry of Finance and the Statistics Division in the Prime Minister's Secretariat of the Prime Minister's
Office, their job being to supervise the statistics work in the
administrative organizations. In 1881 the Statistics Division
of the Prime Minister's Office was raised to the status of
department, and in 1885 to the Cabinet Statistics Bureau of the
Prime Minister. Since the Meiji era it has changed its name
twice. In 1920 it was renamed the Census Department in order
to take the first nationwide census, but in 1922 it was changed
back to the Cabinet Statistics Bureau of the Prime Minister.
Through the preparations and development of the Central Statistics Bureau over the Meiji (1867-1912) and Taisho era (1912-
1925) the statistics system of our country has become integrated.

In 1882 the Statistics Division was set up in each of the
following: the Ministry of Home Affairs, the Ministry of communication and Construction, the Ministry of Navy and the
Ministry of Agriculture and Commerce. By 1885, when at last
the Cabinet Statistics Bureau was established, each administrative organization had set up its own statistics division or
section.

In regard to the actual statistics at that time, these Statistics
Bureaux and departments left the producing of the Statistics to
the care of other departments and they were only involved in the
compilation of the data. This characterizes the early Meiji's
statistics research in the administration. There was, though,
an exception to this, seen in the "Census in KAI Province"
(1879) case. The statistical researches currently conducted
have most of their origins in this period. For example,
"Company Statistics" in 1883, "Statistics for Agriculture,
Forestry and Fishery" in 1884 and "Factory Statistics" in 1909,
were made by the Ministry of Agriculture and Commerce.

By the early Showa era, the Central Statistics Committee established in the Taisho era was still making great contributions
to the improvement and arrangement of the statistics system in
the country. In 1930 the 19th General Meeting of the International Statistics Association was held in Tokyo, which empha-
sized the deep concern felt for statistics. When World War II
set in, the statistics system of our country suffered a substantial jolt as did all other systems. First of all, its advisory
body, the Central Statistics Committee, was abolished in 1940
and in 1942 the Cabinet Statistics Bureau absorbed it into their
Planning Department as an external organ. In such circumstances,
the subjects of the statistical research were restricted.

Moreover, the announcement of the findings was at times inter-
fered with. One example of the government's restriction was
the "Industry Statistics", formerly called "Factory Statistics"
as aforementioned, with a long history of thirty three years,
which was discontinued in 1942.

As Statistics Law was enacted in March 1947 and the statistics
organization in the administration was rearranged, a post-war
structure of the statistics research was systematically established. The law is apparently based on *Rice's Report*, which
was the advice of the "Statistic Mission to Japan" called for
by the General Headquarters of the Allied Powers (GHQ). It was
also considerably influenced by the report of the "Committee
for the Improvement of the Statistics System" submitted to the
government earlier. On receiving this report, the government
established the Statistics Committee in the Prime Minister's
Office. Then the Statistics Committee actively worked on the
Statistics Law contributing to the rebuilding of the statistical
system. In August 1952, when this committee seemed to have
achieved its expected aims, it was abolished. The Statistics
Committee, who made a distinguished contribution to the reorganization of the statistical system, was succeeded by the Statistical Standard Bureau of the Administrative Management Agency.
It is now called the "Commission for Administrative Management
and Inspection" and it serves as the advisory organ.

Present Statistics System and Statistical Organizations

The Statistics Law provides a basis for the statistical research
activity by the statistical organizations of the national and
local governments. It is not designed as a restriction against
nor protection for private statistical research and organizations, as it is designed to apply exclusively to government
statistics. That is to say, the statistical research of the
national and local governments alone are the subject of this
law. The content of the Statistics Law deals mainly with
"Designated Statistics". The Statistics Law was intended to
set the statistical schemes in order and avoid duplication by
placing "Designated Statistics" in the center of the government
statistics system. "Cabinet Order concerning the Scope of the
Statistical Investigation called for Notification", usually
called the "Notified Statistics", was established to deal with
statistical researches other than the "Designated Statistics"
research. In the process of reorganizing statistics research
activity, and along with this law, the Statistical Reports

Coordination Law was introduced in 1952 to check and control
the duplication in statistics research.

Our statistics machinery consists of the following statistics
systems collectively regulated by the Statistics Law and Statistical Reports Coordination Law. The three systems are the
designated statistics system, the notified statistics system
and the statistical report coordination system. Each one of
them will later be explained in detail.

Generally speaking, the government statistics system of a nation
has a wide range of research subjects covering the national and
local governments and its machinery by nature tends to be
centralized. There are, however, some countries in which the
Central Statistics Bureau controls all the statistical research
there is and some that do not. The statistics system of Japan
at present should be termed the decentralized type, which allows
each ministry and agency to perform the statistical research
concerned with their administration on their own. Before World
War II the Cabinet Statistics Bureau had been moving toward the
centralized type of system, putting itself in the position of
the Central Statistics Bureau. After the war the system developed into the decentralized type, for instance, "Vital Statistics" was moved to the Ministry of Health and Welfare, the
ministry concerned. As opposed to the centralized system in
which the Central Statistics Bureau controls the whole statistics
of the government, in the decentralized system the duplication
of statistical research inevitably occurs in each ministry and
agency, for each of them employs the system which links the
statistical research with its own administration. Therefore,
under the previously mentioned Coordination Law they are trying
to avoid such duplications. At any rate, the decentralized
statistics system is inclined to cast a burden upon the public
and local public bodies.

The government statistics structure in Japan is composed of the
national statistical organization and integrated control organizations, branch offices of the government, which work as the
local statistical organization, the local public entities and
the statistics officers in the local area.

The Statistical Research Department is established in the following ministries: the Statistics Bureau of the Prime Minister's
Office, the Ministry of Health and Welfare, the Ministry of
International Trade and Industry, the Ministry of Transport and
the Ministry of Labour. The other ministries also have a Stat-

istics Division which is in charge of statistics. Each of these
departments and divisions is given its own work responsibility
and authority, depending on the laws and regulations of its
ministry. e.g. the Establishment Law of each ministry. The
statistics division of each ministry and agency prepares most
of the Designated Statistics and in regard to the remaining
statistical researches other bureaux and departments concerned
take charge.

The Administrative Inspection Bureau was absorbed into the Administrative Management Agency as the Integrated Control Organization. It was taken into the Administrative Management Agency,
because the Statistics Committee had been abolished. The Administrative Inspection Bureau is in charge of the following:
enforcing the Statistics Law and the Statistical Reports Coordination Law, organizing the statistical establishment, eliminating
duplication in statistical researches and reducing the burden
placed on the general public and on local public bodies.

As for the local statistics organizations, there are some branch
organizations of the government, as follows: the Local Agricultural Administration Bureau, the Statistics Research Office
and the Statistical Research Branch Office of the Ministry of
Agriculture and Forestry, the International Trade and Industry
Bureau and the International Trade and Industry Office of that
Ministry, the Local Government Labour Standards Bureau and the
Labour Standards Inspection of the Ministry of Labour. In the
local governments – municipalities and cities, towns and villages
– the statistics department and the statistics specialist officer
are also present. They are to conduct statistical research of
their own and are authorized or commissioned to take surveys
for the national Government. Therefore, there are two schemes
of statistical research done by the Government and its relating
organizations; one is done directly by each ministry and agency
and the other is done by the commissioned local bodies. Furthermore, within the former scheme there are two kinds, as follows:
one is done exclusively by the national Government and the other
is done through the local branch offices and organizations.
For instance, the various statistics that are applied to the
university and are taken by the Ministry of Education are an
example of the former and an example of the latter is the statistics for agriculture and forestry taken by the branch organizations of the Ministry of Agriculture and Forestry.

However, the statistical research other than Designated Statistics comes to such an enormous amount and the subjects are so

diverse and varied that it eventually causes the research
systems to be of various forms.

DESIGNATED STATISTICS SYSTEM

As we have seen, this designated statistics system is fully
stipulated in its authority, the Statistics Law. The system is
intended to achieve the object of the Statistics Law by assigning
some essential and important statistics to the structure of the
national statistics machinery. It therefore legally approves
many advantages in the statistical researches, and designated
statistics are no doubt the most fundamental statistics in the
nation. In Accordance with Article 2 of the Statistics Law,
designated statistics are defined as follows: "those which have
been prepared by or sponsored by the Government or local public
entity and which have been designated and notified to the public
by the Director-General of the Administrative Management Agency".

Let us observe this system closely and look at the contents in
relation to the definitions in the Statistics Law. The desig-
nation of designated statistics is done by the Director-General
of the Administrative Management Agency, (Article 2 of the Statistics Law). There are no definitions concerning the require-
ments of these statistics, but when preparing the designated
statistics the person conducting the investigation should obtain
in advance the approval of the Director-General of the Administrative Management Agency concerning the following five items:

1. Purpose, items, coverage, data and method.

2. Items to be tabulated and method thereof.

3. Method and data of publication of the results obtained.

4. Method of preserving the documents concerned, and the person
   responsible for it.

5. Estimate of expense, and other matters required by the
   Director-General of the Administrative Management Agency,
   (Article 7)

For the investigation of designated statistics:

A. The Government, the chief of the local public entity or the
   Board of Education may order a person or a juridical person

to report, (Article 5), for the purpose of the investigation of designated statistics.

B. The person conducting the investigation of the designated statistics may request the chief of the administrative organ concerned and others to cooperate on surveying, reporting, etc., (Article 17).

C. The Government may entrust the chief of the local public entity or the Board of Education with a part of the business concerning the investigation of the designated statistics in accordance with the provisions of Cabinet Order, (Article 18).

D. For the purpose of engaging in the business of investigation of the designated statistics, the Prime Minister's Office and each Ministry may have a statistical officer and each local public entity shall have a statistical director, (Article 10).

E. Secret matters of the person, legal person or other bodies found as the result of the investigation of the designated statistics shall be safeguarded, (Article 14).

F. The result of the investigation of the designated statistics shall be published as quickly as possible, (Article 16).

Finally, a person, who fails to make a report or rejects the examination, etc., under the provisions of Article 5 and 13, shall be subject to penal servitude or imprisonment.

That is the essence of the designated statistics system. From above, it can be seen that this statistical investigation enjoys greater protection than any other statistics. Above all, the duty to report, the duty to cooperate and the confidentiality of the investigation, together with the guarantee of the statistical officers, put this system under the best possible conditions. Secondly, it is ordered to publish the results. In other words, this system is formed on the assumption that the result of the investigation should be published, which means that designated statistics are authorized and very important and that it is undoubtedly desirable to have the result published for the public. All the government statistics other than the designated statistics, whether it is the primary statistics or secondary statistics, are not always published, publication being up to the organization concerned. This also shows how

important it is for the statistical results to be made available
to the public.

The designated number of designated statistics, as of the end
of December 1969, is 108. The designated number is given to
each set of statistics in order, therefore, 108 cases of the
statistics have been designated since the establishment of the
Statistics Law. As there are some branch numbers, however,
there are actually 116 cases so far. To list the authoritative
organizations concerned, both the Prime Minister's Office and
the Ministry of Agriculture and Forestry have 22 cases each,
followed by the Ministry of International Trade and Industry -
15 cases, the Ministry of Transport - 9, the Ministry of Education and the Ministry of Health and Welfare - 8 each, the
Ministry of Labour - 7, the Ministry of Construction - 2, the
Ministry of Finance and the Ministry of Home Affairs - 1 each.
The rest include a case of three ministries acting together, 2
cases of two ministries acting together and 16 cases by the
local public entity. In 1968, 58 cases were executed and in
1969, 56 cases. Because of the variety of designated statistics,
such as a single execution, periodicals and non-periodicals,
monthly, annuals and others, the number of the designated statistics executed each year is not the same.

It will be seen, therefore, that the designated statistics
system holds a fundamental position among all other statistics.
It is reasonable to assume that its object is to designate the
most fundamental statistics which have a close connection with
the public and are used for deciding the basic grounds of the
national policy. However, when it comes to the practical work
of the system, they do not seem to be achieving this object
very well.

There are some surveys and investigations among designated statistics whose only purpose is to be published in the Official
Bulletin. For example, when a town wishes to become a city,
just in order to obtain the qualification of the official population, they would have the settled population of the town
designated under Article 254 of the Local Self-Government Law.
This is one of the instances that reveal the simplicity of this
system.

Without doubt, designated statistics since the 1st National
Census, its very beginning, have been a fundamental part of the
whole statistical machinery. As mentioned above, designated
statistics include various surveys that are to be made tempor-

arily or on a "one off" basis. For reference the list of the designated statistics is put in Table 4.

NOTIFIED STATISTICS SYSTEM

The Notified Statistics System is one of the main pillars supporting the statistics machinery. Article 8 of the Statistics Law reads, "in a case of conducting a statistical investigation other than that of designated statistics, the person conducting the investigation shall notify to the Director-General of the Administrative Management Agency" necessary matters such as its purpose, items, scope, data and method, etc. The scope of the notified statistical investigation is defined in the "Cabinet Order concerning the Scope of the Statistical Investigation called for Notification", (Cabinet Order No. 58 of 1950). According to this, it is defined as follows:

1. Statistical investigation concerning land property.

2. Statistical investigation concerning population, households and housing.

3. Statistical investigation concerning prices of commodities and living costs.

4. Statistical investigation concerning public health.

5. Statistical investigation concerning employment or unemployment and wages.

6. Statistical investigation concerning sales of merchandise, purchasing costs and capital of the enterprise.

7. Statistical investigation concerning output, raw materials and consumption of power fuels, and the total stock in storage.

The investigative bodies range from the government, local Public entity, designated metropolis, city, Japan Tobacco and Salt Public Corporation, National Railways, Nippon Telegraph and Telephone Public Corporation, and the Bank of Japan to the Chamber of Commerce and Industry of Japan. In Notified Statistics, some of the public corporations and other minor bodies of the government are included, whereas in designated statistics only the government and local public entities are included.

agency notified years	government		
	new	change	stop
1950	253		
1951	89		
1952	38		
1953	34	1	1
1954	102	4	
1955	141	2	
1956	21	42	12
1957	23	43	
1958	75	14	6
1959	21	36	3
1960	6	7	
1961	25	24	2
1962	29	12	
1963	32	61	5
1964	15	30	
1965	12	19	2
1966	12	12	
1967	12	8	
1968	7	12	5
1969	16	26	
Total	963	343	36

Table 4 The annual transition numbers of the Notified
Statistical Investigations

(This is based on the *Monthly Report on the Designated
Statistics, the Report Coordination and the Notified
Statistics*, vol. 17, no. 12.)

The total number of cases of notified statistical investigations received by the Administrative Management Agency was 4,205 as of the end of 1969. Table 4 displays the annual transition of these cases, specifically done by the government organizations. With the establishment of the Statistical Reports Coordination Law in 1952, resulting from the application of new law to some of the statistical investigations by the national administration, the total number of this kind of investigation has dropped and is still decreasing.

STATISTICAL REPORTS COORDINATION SYSTEM

The Statistical Report Coordination Law is modelled on the Report Control Act enforced in the U.S. The purpose is to relieve the burden imposed in connection with making statistical reports and to contribute to the increase of the efficiency of administrative business by making appropriate coordination of the collection of statistical reports. At the national administrative organs, a large number of statistical investigations other than the already-mentioned designated statistics and notified statistics have been conducted. As these statistical reports vary in their collecting method, report forms and other things, they may too frequently be duplicated and the bodies and persons upon whom they conduct an investigation may also be overburdened. Therefore, the Statistical Reports Coordination Law (Law No. 148 of 1952) was enacted along with the Statistics Law.

According to this law, the national administrative organ should obtain in advance the approval of the Director-General of the Administrative Management Agency if the statistical report they ask for is to be submitted by persons, juridical persons or other organizations totalling ten or more. During the enforcement of the Statistical Reports Coordination Law from May 1952 until the end of 1969, cases that were approved by the Administrative Management Agency totalled 7,300. Its annual transition is shown on Table 5. Because the same statistical investigation can be counted several times due to its procedure, the figures on Table 5 are not quite accurate, nevertheless, we can get an idea of the trend.

BIBLIOGRAPHY:

1.   Japan Statistical Institute, ed., *The Development*

Years	Number
1952	79
1953	272
1954	381
1955	556
1956	310
1957	331
1958	359
1959	292
1960	433
1961	346
1962	469
1963	527
1964	444
1965	434
1966	440
1967	553
1968	502
1969	572
TOTAL	7,300

Table 5   The Annual Transition Numbers of the
Report Coordination

(This is based on *The Monthly Report on the
Designated Statistics, the Report Coordination
and The Notified Statistics,* vol. 17, no. 12)

History of Statistics in Japan, Tokyo, University of Tokyo Press, 1960, 310 p.

2. UTSUMI, Koichiro, ed., *Statistics*, Tokyo, Yuuhikaku, 1966, 283 p.

3. ARISAWA, Hiromi, ed., *Statistics*, Tokyo, Mainichi Newspaper Company, 1955, 362 p.

4.   Government Publications and Copyright

Government publications, published by government organizations vary a great deal in content, form and publishing methods. This section aims to explain how these government publications are treated as regards the Copyright Law.

The copyright system of our country was germinated in the Publication Act of 1869, where the protection of copyright can be seen. Later in 1893 the Literary Property Law was established but it was not until 1897 that the Copyright Law was enacted and the people began to be provided with the modern copyright system. In the same year, Japan signed the Bern Treaty for the Protection of Literary and Artistic Works, which is an international copyright protection treaty. With the development of means of utilizing the publication and the revision of the international treaty, the Copyright Law has been partially amended several times. From 1962 the Ministry of Education started to work on the full revision of the Copyright Law. On April 28, 1970, the New Copyright Law eventually passed the Diet. This New Copyright Law (Law No. 48), the existing Copyright Law, was promulgated on May 6th and carried into effect on 1st January 1971. The New Copyright Law, which should also be called the amended Copyright Law, is well suited to the present situation and also meets the standard of the latest Treaty of Bern. However, Japan only signed the Amended Treaty of Rome in 1928 and has never joined in, for example, the Amended Treaty of Brussels (1948) and the Amended Treaty of Stockholm in 1967, although the latter has not yet become effective, for less than five countries have signed it.

The copyright system underwent a renewal, when the new law was enacted. We will now examine the copyright problem in regard to government publications under the new law and compare the old and new law in regard to this problem.

WORKS OF GOVERNMENT ORGANIZATIONS

Copyright is a legalized right of the author. The object
protected by this copyright is called the works. The kind and
scope of the works vary widely. Generally, however, the following things are included in the works: linguistic, artistic,
musical and architectural works, diagrams, films and pictures,
derivative works and edited publications. It is prescribed by
law that these works should be protected.

However, news of the day and miscellaneous facts having the
characteristic of mere items of information do not fall within
the term "works". Accordingly, all the works produced by the
staff and organizations of the government that are included in
the examples of works are subject to the protection. There are,
however, some works among those of the government organizations
which are not protected. The following are the ones that do
not form the subject matter of the rights provided for in
Chapter II, Rights of Authors.

> *Works not protected* (Article 13 of the New Copyright
> Law):
>
> 1. The Constitutions and other laws and regulations.
>
> 2. Notifications, instructions, circular notices and
>   the like issued by organs of the State or local
>   public entities.
>
> 3. Judgements, decisions, orders and decrees of law
>   courts, as well as rulings and decisions made by
>   administrative organs in proceedings similar to
>   judicial ones.

(1) corresponds to Article 11 of the old law. It includes
treaties, laws, Cabinet orders, ministerial ordinances and
regulations, or the rules and regulations of the local public
entity, besides the Constitutions.

(2) and (3) correspond to Article 11, the Official Documents in
the old law. This "Official Documents" however, has been
criticized in that its scope and content were not clear. The
official documents were understood to be the documents made by
the public agencies for their public business, which included
the announcements, instructions, notifications, ordinances,
notes, proceedings and decisions of the court and the like.

But when they used the term "official documents", it could possibly be misunderstood in that all the works of the public agencies were somehow the same as the official documents that have no copyright. Some people also wondered how they should treat the various white papers, reports and the like published by the government. Consequently, in the new law they did not use the term "official documents" and in order to make this point clear, they prescribed each item in detail in (2) and (3). The new law also excludes translations and compilations of statutes and judicial cases and the like which are prepared by the government and the local public entity, and are mentioned in (1) through (3). Although these works fulfil the required conditions of copyright, they are left out, because it is very important that they are utilized by the public, for the public benefit in that it is essential for the public to be familiar with them.

Concerning the limitations on copyright, it is prescribed that "it shall be permissible to make quotations from a work already made public, provided that it is compatible with fair practice and their extent does not exceed that justified by purposes such as news reporting, criticism or research". (Article 32 paragraph 2 of the New Copyright Law). It is thus, one of the new law's characteristics to acknowledge free and broader exploitation of works such as reports and research papers.

Moreover, with regard to the exploitation of political speeches (Article 40), they also permit its exploitation as much as possible, though they put it under their protection. In other words, they permit the exploitation except for the compilation of a certain person, prescribing that "it shall be permissible to exploit, by any means, political speeches delivered in public and speeches delivered in the course of judicial proceedings, except when such exploitation involves a collection of the works of a single author" (Article 40 paragraph 1). Also, "it shall be permissible to reproduce in the press, broadcast and diffuse by wire, speeches not falling within the preceding paragraph, which are delivered in public in organs of the State or local public entities" (Article 40 paragraph 2).

In Japan the Copyright Law provides protection for the works of government organizations, but some countries do not give protection for them, for example, they are not protected by the law in the U.S.

AUTHOR OF THE GOVERNMENT PUBLICATIONS

The author means one who creates his work. It does not mean he
is always alone. There are works called joint works that are
created by more than one author, and corporate works that are
created by some organization or corporate body.

The government produces many works made by government organizations and their staff. These are usually called corporate works
or works under a corporate name in order to make a distinction
between these works and works produced by individuals. To name
a few kinds of corporate works among the government publications
from the authorship point of view;(1) the works produced by
officials on their official duties (Official Duty Works),(2) the
works produced by a third person who was asked to do a said job
by the government organization (Entrusted Works), and (3) compilations of the works made by the government organizations themselves, or of the existing works (Compilations).

Official Duty Works

There have been a few interpretations and problems over who the
author is to be when staff of the government or a company
produce a work. Speaking from the viewpoint of copyright principle, it would be reasonably judged that the creator of the
work should possess the premier copyright. Therefore, the
copyright should belong to the person who writes the work even
if it is for the purpose of his official duty. On the other
hand, there is another viewpoint that whoever owns the copyright,
the corporate body as well as the individual, can as a legal
party be considered the author. In this case, whenever a person
writes a work for the State or corporate body simply as one of
his duties, or when ordered to do so by the State, the State or
the corporate body to which he belongs owns the copyright.

The old law made no reference to this point. It was commonly
accepted, however, that authorship of works produced as an
official duty should belong to the State or corporate body who
employed the staff to write them. It was stipulated and made
clear in Article 15 of the new law, in which they define the
authorship of a work made under the name of a legal person,
etc., that "the authorship of a work which, on the initiation
of a legal person or other employer (hereinafter in this Article
referred to as 'legal person, etc.'), is made by his employee
in the course of his duties and is made public under the name

of such legal person, etc. as the author shall be attributed to
that legal person, etc., unless otherwise stipulated in a contract, work regulation or the like in force at the time of the
making of the work" (Article 15). In short, it is to be considered that the State itself stands as the author. The subject
of both moral rights and copyright is assumed to be the State.
Accordingly, the required conditions are strictly defined. The
following are these necessary conditions:

1. The State as an employer should take the initiative in
    planning and other things for the work.

2. The work is made by the official in the course of his duties.

3. Having no special agreement made between the State and the
    employee, the work is formed by a harmonious contribution
    of each official employee.

4. The State should publish it and make it public on its own
    responsibility.

They are very important conditions. It should be assumed that,
unless defined in a contract or in particular work regulations,
the copyright goes to the official when he produces the work on
account of his official duties and makes it public under his
own name. Such activities of officials in the national government are most remarkable, ranging from magazines to books. It
is unnecessary to say that if a work is not made for one's
official duties, no one can have control over it. Most of these
government officials, however, make works such as, among other
things, the commentary on the revised law on the basis of the
knowledge they obtained in the course of their duties. In such
a case, it is prescribed in the Copyright Law that both moral
rights and copyright belong to the official. After all, to
have the knowledge obtained in the course of one's duties should
not be the most vital condition for those official duty works.

Entrusted Works

Among the works of the government organizations, there are not
only those that are made by its officials but also ones made by
others. They often entrust officials from the field concerned
or some specialists who are non-officials with work that requires
expert knowledge. That is what we call entrusted works. In
regard to these, on the principle that the moral rights and

copyright belong to the creator of the work, the individual should possess all of the rights. This would, however, only apply unless otherwise specified in the contract. It is right and proper that the government organizations exploit the work for their original purpose, however, the scope of exploitation should stay within the limit provided in the contract. Further, the point as to whether the copyright is transferred to the government or the rights of exploitation and publication are taken over by the government and the like should be referred to in the contract.

As for the entrusted works, it is interpreted that no matter how different a contract each may have, the moral rights of the work belong to the person who made the work. The moral rights consist of the following: the right of making the work public, the right of determining the indication of the author's name and the right of preserving integrity. In the old law, it was prescribed that no modification should be added to the work without asking the person who made it. On the other hand, in the new law it says that "the author shall have the right to preserve the integrity of his work and its title against any distortion, mutilation or other modification against his will" (Article 20).

Compilations

As we have already seen in "the works not protected", some compilations, made by the State and local public entities, such as laws and regulations, cannot form the subject matter of protection. However, the compilations other than the above-mentioned could form the subject matter of the rights and, there-fore, the State and the local entities could be the author. In the new law it is prescribed that "compilations which, by reason of the selection and arrangement of their contents, constitute intellectual creations shall be protected as indepen-dent works" (Article 12). Compilations made by the national government organizations, comprising both compilations of works and of non-works, are very numerous.

EXPLOITATION OF THE WORKS OF GOVERNMENT ORGANIZATIONS

The copyright provides for the exploitation of the works. In other words, the copyright owner may grant another person author-ization to exploit the work for, among other things, publishing

and broadcasting. There are two methods by which the government organizations publish their works or compilations.

The first one is that they personally publish them, which ties
in with the spirit of the Copyright Law that "the author shall
have the exclusive right to reproduce his work" (Article 21).
The majority of the government publications are thus issued from
each government organization. It is at this point that the
government publications are different from the works of individuals. Most of the latter use another method in which they
leave the publishing to the publishing company. It is rarely
the case that the individual would publish his work at his own
expense. This characteristic of government publications in
which the government organization itself, as the author, publishes the works is derived from the make-up of government
publications. The administrative reports, official business
reports and other similar reports, are the result of the
enforcement of government policy, which the government as the
administrator is obliged to make public. These works should
as a rule be distributed free of charge and that is the reason
why the government has traditionally published themselves.

There is the Printing Bureau in the Ministry of Finance which
is the printing and publishing organization for the works of
government organizations. It is a distinctive institution that
functions as a central publishing organization by printing and
publishing the works of each organization in the government.
For example, at the Printing Bureau they compile, print and
publish the Official Gazette, statute books and other government publications.

The other method is to have the third party publish their works
for them. The government publications published by a private
publishing company or an outer organization fall under this
category. In such a case, the contract on exploitation would
be made between the government organizations and the publishing
company just as in the case of a regular publication. Establishing the right of publication, they enter into the contract
on publishing. Works of the State that are intangible assets
would be treated in the same way as the tangible assets. The
contents of the publication contract may vary according to the
characteristics of the works. The "Law concerning the Rights
of Publication and Others for the Texts by the Ministry of
Education" (Law No. 149, 1949), for instance, is the law that
stipulates the contract. In conclusion, the practice of the
publishing contract should be carried out as due recognition

that these works could be the subject of profit.

Now in regard to the conditions required for the author to
receive legal protection as a copyright owner, there exist the
following two systems. One is called formulism which requires
the regular procedures such as the registration, copyright
deposit and the indication of the copyright. The other is
called non-formulism, which does not require any procedures.
In a word, whenever an author creates a work, he would immediately be provided with a copyright. The member nations of the
Bern Treaty, including Japan, England, France and Germany, adopt
the latter system. Until 1899 when Copyright Law was enacted
and Japan signed the Bern Treaty, Japan had taken the formulism
system. Therefore, before that time when the government wanted
to register the copyright for their works, they would have to
go through due formalities, which were nevertheless more simple
than that for regular publications.

Term of Protection

The purpose of the term of protection against the copyright
stipulated has two aspects; one is to protect the copyright
owner's interests in his assets, while the other is to impose
restrictions on the copyright in the interests of the public.
It is in the public interest that the duration is not infinite.
Accordingly, anybody can exploit the work when a certain period
of time after the creation of the work has elapsed. The duration
depends on the kind and nature of the work. In the New Copyright Law the duration was changed to a period of fifty years
after the death of the author, following the general trend in
the world. In the old law, through several revisions, it was
stipulated that the duration for the regular publications was
to be thirty years after the death of the author, and for the
works under the name of a corporate body was to be thirty three
years after the publication of the work, and for the photographic
works thirteen years after the publication of the work. Until
recently, however, the duration for many years had been set for
thirty years. From 1962 when they began to revise the law,
they made four provisional amendments before 1970. Meanwhile,
the duration was extended to a period of thirty eight years.

Government publications are mostly published under the name of
the corporate body. As death never occurs to the State and the
legal body, it is impossible to use the term "after the death
of the author" for them. Therefore, it is prescribed in the

law as "after the making public of the work". The new law
defines that the duration for works bearing the name of a corporate body should last "until the end of a period of fifty years
following the making public of the work" (Article 53 paragraph
1). The duration is to be counted from 1st January of the new
year following the author's death, or the making public. The
works whose duration of protection has once expired, by all
rights, cannot be protected again. Consequently, even though
the duration of protection was extended to a period of fifty
years in the new law, those which have no valid duration cannot
be renewed.

With regard to the free exploitation of the works of government
organizations, it has been already mentioned as one included
with the works not protected. When any of the government organizations intend to exploit someone's work, they usually take
the same step as all other people. They ask the copyright
owner to grant them authorization to exploit his work. Although
it is permissible to reproduce the work in school textbooks,
textbooks authorized by the Ministry of Education or those that
are compiled under the authorship of the Ministry of Education,
they are bound to go through due formalities and pay compensation
to the copyright owner.

The points at issue in respect to free exploitation are in
Article 42 of the New Copyright Law, which stipulates the reproduction for judicial proceedings, etc. It takes the view which
had been inserted into the old law at the revision of 1934.
In the old law it was prescribed that "it is permissible to
reproduce a work exclusively in the service of the government
organizations" and reproducing a work which had been already
published was not to be regarded as a spurious work (Article
30 paragraph 1-9 of the old law). In regard to the policy of
the law, which is supposed to respect the copyright of the
individual, it has been said that one should be discreet in
applying this stipulation. The new law acknowledging the free
exploitations defines its scope clearly by placing restrictions
on it. That is, "it shall be permissible to reproduce a work
if and to the extent deemed necessary for the purpose of judicial
proceedings and of internal use in legislative or administrative
organs, provided that such reproduction does not unreasonably
prejudice the interests of the copyright owner in the light of
the nature and the purpose of the work as well as the number of
copies and the character of reproduction" (Article 42 of the
New Copyright Law). The work can be reproduced only in a small
number of copies for the purpose of internal use. It is also

not permissible to reproduce the work in order to distribute it to all the officials in the organ as reference data. It should be understood that it is not permitted to reproduce a great number of copies to be distributed outside by reason of administrative necessity.

BIBLIOGRAPHY:

1. YAMAMOTO, Keiichi, *Copyright Law* (Complete Works of Jurisprudence 54-II), Tokyo, Yuuhikaku, 1969, 289 p.

2. Copyright Division, Cultural Affairs Department, Agency for Cultural Affairs, *Facts about the New Copyright Law* (Copyright Series No. 14), Tokyo, 1970, 102 p.

3. SANO, Bunichiro and Toshio Suzuki, *Questions and Answers on the New Copyright Law*, Tokyo, Shinjidaisha, 1970, 480 p.

4. KAMIIDE, Hichiro, "Public Documents and Copyright No. 1", *Monthly Catalogue of Government Publications* 6:7, Tokyo, 1962.

5. —————, "Public Documents and Copyright No. 2", *Monthly Catalogue of Government Publications* 6:8, Tokyo, 1962.

PART II

PUBLICATION AND DISTRIBUTION OF GOVERNMENT PUBLICATIONS

CHAPTER 1
PUBLISHING ORGANIZATIONS OF GOVERNMENT
PUBLICATIONS

1. Publication of Government Publications in Europe
    and the U.S.

Before observing the publication organization in Japan, let us
briefly look at the printing and publishing of government publications in Europe and the U.S.

As we have seen, government publications are different in terms
of printing, publishing and distribution from other publications,
this being one of their characteristics. The processes followed
in publishing them depends on the country. There are four types
of publishing systems according to the printing and publishing
methods each country undertakes. For the first type, the government structure is so designed that all the printing and publishing of government publications is done collectively by a special
organization of the government. For the second type, they have
separate organizations of printing and publishing, each of them
being exclusively in charge of their respective field. As
regards the third type, it is either the printing organization
that collectively executes the printing and then each ministry
and agency individually executes the publishing, or the printing
is done individually at each organization while the publishing
is done collectively. For the fourth type, there is not any
established system of printing and publishing in the government
structure, therefore, each organization independently prints
and publishes on their own. The second type, though, can be
regarded as very similar to the first if there can be any connection and collaboration between the printing and publishing
organization.

Some of the countries which belong to the first type are the
U.S., England, Canada, Italy and the Netherlands. It is also
called the Anglo-American type, for they represent this type.
Countries of the second type are India and Pakistan. Austria

and Denmark belong to the third type. The fourth type includes
France, West Germany, Belgium, Spain, Sweden and Japan.

The characteristic of the first type is that it is advantageous
for controlling the whole system, making a rational catalogue
and effective distribution owing to the collective operation of
printing, publishing and distribution. In regard to the second
and third types, if the publishing is done collectively,
centralized control is possible. The fourth type, also called
the Continental type, has the characteristic of the decentralized system of printing and publishing, therefore, even though
they have the printing or publishing organization within the
Government, they cannot function too well. It is commonly
agreed that the first is systematically superior to the others.

Government Publications Publishing in England and the U.S.

The following are examples of the collective printing and
publishing system of Government publications in England and the
U.S.

ENGLAND

Let us look at the system in England. They have Her Majesty's
Stationery Office, the central organization for printing and
publishing, which was established in 1786. At first they were
mainly in charge of supplying stationery for the Government
organizations, but in the 19th century it became the publishing
organization for government publications. At that time, though,
they did not print them and it was in the 20th century that
they began to do so. Today it is one of the biggest publishing
establishments including the commercial publishing companies in
England.

They have a system that all the processes from printing to distributing and marketing are controlled and supervised by Her
Majesty's Stationery Office. In other words, almost all the
government publications, but for a few exceptions, are published
by Her Majesty's Stationery Office and sold through its sales
organization. Generally speaking, when the open documents of
the government are to be published by the government organization, Her Majesty's Stationery Office decides its publication
after examining the sales value of the publication both from
the public utility and commercial benefit viewpoints. Then
they decide the number of the publication to be published and

they print and publish them according to the form each publication requires. As soon as they are ready they are put on the
market of the Book Shop and the Sales Agency of Her Majesty's
Stationery Office throughout the country.

They now publish about 6,000 kinds of government publications
annually. As a rule, the parliamentary publications are
printed by Her Majesty's Stationery Office, but the non-
parliamentary publications are printed by commercial printing
companies. However, some non-parliamentary publications that
are similar in character to the parliamentary publications are
supposed to be printed at Her Majesty's Stationery Office,
provided that they are to be printed or published by a certain
date. On the basis of the Gretton Committee Report, one third
of all the printing demands are kept so that they can be available for the printing of parliamentary publications, secret
documents, and other important publications. Accordingly, the
printing of the non-parliamentary publications is entrusted to
about 2,000 registered commercial printers.

The Central Office of Information, the Patent Office, the
Ordinance Survey and the Admiralty Hydrographic Department are
allowed to publish their own publications to suit the government's convenience.

Each office of the Government also publishes on its own a percentage of the government publications which are distributed
free of charge. They are said to be numerous but as they are
not under bibliographical control, it is difficult to get hold
of the actual figures.

U.S.A.

In the U.S. the Government Printing Office established in 1860
is in charge of printing, publishing and distributing. From
the beginning, the Government Printing Office started as the
central printing office, then in 1895, when the Printing Act
was enacted, printing and distributing became centralized.
When the Superintendent of Documents of the Government Printing
Office took over the business that had been done by the Department of Interior in 1895, it began to be regarded as the central
printing and publishing organization.

They make it a principle that the Government Printing Office
puts out the publications for the Congress, courts, and the
administration. Actually, however, though at one time the

Government Printing Office published all the Government publications, they usually do not publish every single Government
publication. According to the Merritt Report, which surveyed
Government publications every ten years from 1900 to 1940, the
percentage of Government publications that were published by
the Government Printing Office reached a peak in 1900 with
52.8 per cent but from then on gradually decreased to 21.8 per
cent in 1940. Based on the presumption made by the Joint
Committee on Printing of 1962, it is now said to be around 35
to 40 per cent. But this high rate of non-Government Printing
Office publications disturbs the concentrated control system
and prevents it from being fully effective.

The traits of the U.S. system can be found in their method of
distribution and provision. Government publications in the U.S.
are distributed free of charge and also sold to the general public. In regard to the free distribution, in our country as in
many other countries they are mainly distributed to a limited
number of the general public and to the groups and bodies concerned. In the U.S. and Canada, however, on the basis of the
law, they set up depository libraries for Government publications
in which anybody can utilize the Government publications. This
depository library system was put in practice under the charge of
the Government Printing Office. It serves both utilization and
maintenance of the Government publications. In this system, two
libraries for an election district for the Congress are appointed
by the House of Representatives and two other libraries for each
state are appointed by the House of Senate. They include not
only public libraries but also university libraries. These
appointed libraries are supplied with Government publications by
the Superintendent of Documents of the Government Printing Office,
and the publications are used by the libraries and the public in
the region. A regional depository library is also set up in
each state where they permanently preserve the Government publications, provide reference service, and a loan system between the
libraries in the region. There are 961 depository libraries in
the U.S. as of 1968. Under the Amended Depository Library Act,
they are allowed to appoint as many as 1328 libraries. Thus in the
U.S. they enforce the centralized control system.

2.   The Publishing of Government Publications in Japan

The type of printing and publishing done in Japan is the Continental type. Above all, it resembles the French system, that
is, it is the dual structure. While having the Government

printing organization, each organization of the Government puts
out publications on its own.

The Printing Bureau of the Ministry of Finance was established
as the Government printing organization in Japan. As it will
be observed in detail later, it has developed into a central
organ of printing and publishing for the Government publications
since the Meiji era.   However, it has never functioned as the
central printing and publishing organization seen in the Anglo-
American type. In 1927 there appeared a movement to centralize
the system, making the Printing Bureau print and publish all
the Government publications. But it only dealt with the compilation and publication of the *Catalogue of Books of the Government Organizations* and did not bear fruit. After the war, in
the process of arranging the government publications "diffusion
system" which originated from R.P. Dore's Proposal in 1956,
there were some opportunities to bring forth centralized control
but it did not come about.

Therefore, they now depend on the present system. The Printing
Bureau appeals to each ministry and agency urging them to
utilize the Printing Bureau when printing and publishing government publications but there are no strong regulations to compel
them to do so, and usually only the white papers are published
at the Printing Bureau. On the other hand, the Government
publications that are published by each ministry and agency on
their own are put out freely and in quite large quantities.

There is a report which says that the Printing Bureau of the
Ministry of Finance prints only thirty per cent of all Government publications. However, judging from the statistics which
show that the number of Government publications put out in 1969
was only 180, it could be presumed that the percentage would
actually be even lower. It means that most publications are
dependent upon each ministry's own publishing.

Now let us take a close look at the publishing done by each
ministry and agency. One of the main reasons they put out their
own publications is that the Printing Bureau, unlike Her
Majesty's Stationery Office in England, enforces the self-
supporting accounting system. In other words, each ministry
has the cost of its own printing and publishing in its budget.
Therefore, each of them at its own discretion usually prints
and publishes the publications at commercial publishing
companies or the extra-governmental organizations. There are
47 units of the organ such as ministry, office, agency, bureau

and committee in the national government, and altogether 1,025 units of departments which are the sources of information. However, among them there are only a couple of independent publishing departments that deal with the printing and publishing companies, therefore, as a rule each accounting section in the organization is in charge of the publishing business.

In fact, these smaller sections are the subject for the publishing operation. The publishing should be done on the assumption that it is a mission demanded by the public and at the same time that it pays. Though all the Government publications in a way ought to be distributed to the public free of charge, it is not feasible because of many limiting factors. Thus there are various forms and types of publications. The following are major types of publications done by the ministry and agency.

1. The publishing is done at the expense of the ministry leaving printing and publishing to the commercial publishing company.

2. Besides the publication being done and paid for by the ministry, they have the same publication published by the commercial publishing company for public sale.

3. The ministry compiles or edits the work and lets the commercial publishing company publish it.

These different systems are chosen depending upon the purpose and budget of the publication. In many cases, when the budget is tight the ministry buys a certain number of the publications that are published by the extra-governmental organization or the commercial publishing company even though the ministry is the author of it. When the ministry publishes two of the same kinds of publication, one published by themselves and another by the commercial company, they sometimes buy the one on the market.

Now let us look at the commercial publishing company and the extra-governmental organizations which print and publish the government publications. According to the survey done by the National Diet Library[1], there are 580 of these groups and companies. As of February 1969 the publications put out by them amounted to 1,800 annually. Half of these 580 companies are quite active in publishing the Government publications. One tenth of these 580 are most active, which eventually comprise the "Liaison Meeting of the Diffusion and Enforcement of Government Publications". The following are the 30 members of which it is composed.

They are: Asian Economic Publishing Co., Council of Transport Investigation, Gakuyo Shobo, Construction Documents Co., Kosei Publishing Co., Association of Health and Welfare Statistics, Jichi Nippo Co., Social Insurance Laws and Regulations Research Institute, Heavy Industry Cooperation, Business Laws and Regulations Research Institute, New Japan Statute Publishing, Fishery Co., Tax Research Institute, Cooperative Association of Oil Industry Newspaper Co., Daiichi Hoki Publishing Co., Taisei Publishing Co., Council of Local Finance, Research Council of Small and Medium Enterprise, Trade and Industry Research Co., Research Council of Trade and Industry, Gyosei Ltd., Nippon Kajo Publishing, Japan Trusted Investigation, Sales Centre of Japanese Laws and Regulations Form, Association of Agriculture and Forestry Statistics, Hara Shobo, Medical Publishing Co., Ratisu, Association of Laws and Regulations.

Observing these active groups, we find that they are mostly comprised of the companies of the laws and regulations publications and some associations, the extra-governmental organizations, and only a few general publishing companies. Unquestionably the former two are greatly concerned with the Government, but many other general companies besides them are widely involved in publishing the Government publications nowadays.

NOTES:

> 1. National Diet Library, *List of the Publications compiled and edited by the State and published by the Government related Bodies and the Companies*, Tokyo, 1969, p. 175.

BIBLIOGRAPHY:

> 1. ISHII, Goro, "Government Publications in England No. 1 and No. 2", *Monthly Catalogue of Government Publications* 5:6, 7, Tokyo, 1961.
>
> 2. TANABE, Yoshitaro, "Various Problems concerning the Government Publications and their Catalogues", (Studies of Library Series No. 3) ed. by the National Diet Library.

3. KUROKI, Tsutomu, "The Depository Library System in
    the U.S.", *Bulletin of the National College of
    Library Science*, vol. 1, Tokyo, 1966, pp. 75-80.

4. SCHMECKEBIER, Laurence F., *Government Publications
    and their Use*, 2nd ed., Washington, The Brookings
    Institution, 1969, 502 p.

5. OLL'É, James G., *An Introduction to British Govern-
    ment Publications*, London, Association of Assistant
    Librarians, 1965, 128 p.

3.   Printing Bureau of the Ministry of Finance

HISTORY OF THE PRINTING BUREAU OF THE MINISTRY OF FINANCE

Let us briefly observe the history of the Printing Bureau. It
started as the Paper Money Office that was established within
the Ministry of Finance on 27th July 1871. On 11th August of
the same year it was combined with the Bureau of Typewriting,
starting typographical printing. On 10th December 1878, it was
named the Printing Bureau. On 1st November 1898 it was united
with the Official Gazette Bureau of the Cabinet, taking over
the information business relating to the *Official Gazette*, and
became the Printing Bureau for the extra-ministerial bureau of
the Cabinet. Then in accordance with the revision of the regulations governing the organizations, it became the Printing
Bureau inside the Cabinet on 22nd December 1924. As soon as
the "Policy for the Enforcement of the Domestic System" was
passed in the Cabinet Council, during the tense situation of
the war, the Printing Bureau returned to the Ministry of Finance
as its extra-ministerial bureau after some 45 years of being a
separate organ. After World War II in conformity with the
Establishment Law of the Ministry of Finance, it became the
Printing Agency on 1st June 1949. When the law was revised, it
was changed to the Printing Bureau, an auxiliary organ of the
Ministry of Finance.

DEVELOPMENT OF THE PUBLISHING

The business of the Printing Bureau falls into two main categories; the printing of bills and bonds, and the publishing of
books and the like. Here we will outline the latter.

As can be seen, the original purpose of the Paper Money Office
was to unify the circulation of money and the state economy, by
issuing paper money and public bonds and securities. At that
time printing, in general, in Japan was immature and poor in
quality, as they tried to imitate the Western printing introduced
shortly before. Consequently, in some cases, when they could
not have it done in Japan, they had to have it done in Germany.
The structure of the Meiji government was also not settled or
definite, and repeatedly they reorganized and transferred the
ministries. It affected the Printing Bureau, too, when the
production of postage stamps was transferred to the Paper Money
Office in January 1872. In regard to the printing and issuing
of governmental documents, the Bureau of Printing was established
in the Cabinet on 20th September 1872, which was the printing,
publishing and distributing organization for Government publications. This act revealed the innovative attitude of the Meiji
government toward government publications and embodied their
ideas[1] They were trying to set up a centralized printing and
publishing organization modelled on the Western style, by
inheriting the printing machines from the Ministry of the Navy
and the Ministry of Education and by combining the printing
office of the Ministry of Technology. However, they had barely
started to develop it before .the Bureau of Printing was integrated into the Paper Money Office on 4th September 1875. Then
the Paper Money Office was renamed the Bureau of Typography,
where most confidential documents were printed. Thus it became
the Printing Bureau in 1878.

In regard to publication, the *Journal of the Cabinet* was
published by the Bureau of Printing until its abolition in
January 1877, which was followed by the publication of the
Official Gazette in March 1882. In May 1883 they established
the Bureau of Documents and published the first *Official Gazette*
on 2nd July, 1883. In the period from 1886 to 1890 it was
suspended sporadically because of the transfer of the printing
office. In 1891 they started to print it again at the Official
Gazette Printing Bureau. It was in 1898 that all the work for
the *Official Gazette*, from compilation to publishing, finally
began to be done at the Official Gazette Bureau of the Cabinet,
the Official Gazette Office of the Printing Bureau. This publication of the *Official Gazette* has played a most important part
in the world of publishing.

The *Statute Book* was published in the early period as well as
the *Official Gazette*. From August 1886, it began to be put out
by the Printing Bureau. However, as mentioned above, during

the time from 1886 to 1893 it was printed and published at the Official Gazette Bureau, for printing other than money and stamps had to be carried out at the same place as the *Official Gazette*. During that period, therefore, they published the *Statute Book* and *Personnel Directory* as the supplement of the *Official Gazette*.

The *Personnel Directory* appeared for the first time on 27th December 1886 and was published by the Printing Bureau. It seems to have been published earlier by the ministry and agency individually, for we find it in the first Report of the Typography Department of the Printing Bureau (1877). From 1894 up to the present, it has been published in book form instead of as the supplement of the *Official Gazette*.

With respect to the Proceedings of the Diet, the *Official Gazette* for the first time published the Stenographical Minutes of the Imperial Diet of 2nd December 1890, but from the next edition of the Minutes until now, it has been published as the extra-edition of the *Official Gazette*.

The Printing Bureau set up a branch office in the Ministry of Education when they printed the text books compiled by the Ministry of Education from 1889 to 1890. Then they expanded their printing operation to print, among other things, *Historical Records of Great Japan*, and the *Palaeography of Great Japan*[2].

In the Taisho era, "the general news column" was added to the *Official Gazette* from 7th April 1922. It was very similar to the present *Current Topics Review* in form and in content and had PR type of information.

It was natural that they published in line with the domestic policy from 1926 to 1945. The government decided on the National Spirits Mobilization Enforcement Policy in 1939 and also the Order of Temporary Control for Speech, Publishing and Meeting in 1941. Accordingly, the Printing Bureau was engaged in publishing a collection of books with a teaching-text tendency such as the *Duty of the National, Basic Principle of National Policy, Library of Teaching, A Series of the Japanese Spirit, Outline of the National Morality,* and *Reader of National Education*. Most of these ran through 6 to 7 impressions and more than a million copies each were put out.

In 1936 the general news was superceded by the *Weekly Review of Events* founded on 14th October. The circumstances of this are

explained by Tsuchiya, then Director of the Printing Bureau, in
his *From General News to Weekly Review of Events* as follows:
"as the conditions of society have become many and diverse, we
are afraid that the present general news might fall short of
everyone's expectation. Therefore, in order to expand and
develop it, we have decided to change the name and form
altogether and have come to publish it as the *Weekly Review of
Events*, the supplement of the *Official Gazette*, in a half size
of the *Official Gazette*.(3)" Its contents included the following:
(1) explanation of the laws and regulations, (2) explanation of
various policies, (3) the domestic and foreign world's events
in general and (4) economics, art and science. Presently with
the China Incident and the growing tension in the world, it was
changed from the supplement to an independent weekly, which
eventually became the government PR magazine propagandizing for
the Intelligence Division of the Cabinet. It was finally made
into the pamphlet of state policy contributing to the National
Mobilization Movement and the Decisive-Battle-for-all-the-
Hundred-Million propagandas. They then published 1.5 million
copies each week, as they set the goal at one copy per household throughout the nation.

The *Photograph Weekly* was also published from February 1938 as
a companion volume to the *Weekly Review of Events*. Its purpose
was to make the *Weekly Review of Events* clearer and more effective by using photographs. They published 500,000 copies
weekly. Both the *Weekly Review of Events* and the *Photograph
Weekly* were abolished on 11th July, 1945.

Thus the Printing Bureau was enthusiastically involved with
propaganda activity, especially between 1935 to 1945, as a
result of state policy. As of 1943, 25 kinds of publications
were put out by the Printing Bureau, including the *Official
Gazette, Weekly Review of Events, Photograph Weekly, Statute
Book, Catalogue of Books of the Government Organization,
Research on the Population Problem, Personnel Directory, Labour
Statistics Monthly, Ministry of Education Annual, Handbook of
the Conditions of the World Powers* and *Japan-International
Trade Annual*. Out of all of them four were compiled and published by the Printing Bureau. They also printed about 150
kinds of books on teaching and on various laws and regulations.

Undergoing complete change after the war, they started to
publish from a democratic and pacifist viewpoint. At that time
the Printing Bureau was not restored to its previous form and
was under the control of the General Headquarters of the Allied

Powers, therefore, the government had to obey the orders of the Allied Powers and do whatever they said. In pressing for democracy in Japan, one of the means the GHQ used was to publish and diffuse a series of books on social education activating the Social Education Bureau of the Ministry of Education as its nucleus and the Federation of Social Education as its propulsive force.

Beginning from 1947, many books on social education such as the *School Class Library, New Book of Women, New Book of Young Men,* and *Citizen's Library* and *Community Center Series* for the general public were successively published. The Printing Bureau was asked to aid in the printing and distributing of these books and then printed them extensively. In regard to the distribution, besides the local sales agency for the Official Gazette, they made it a system to give copies to the chief of the Documents Section in each prefectural government in charge of the diffusion of Government publications. Later they changed it from the Documents Section Chief to the chief of the Social Education Section. At any rate, after 1950 the activities of the Printing Bureau and the Education Bureau became insignificant, they had fulfilled their duty of publishing books for the sake of democracy.

Around 1949 indications of the stabilized situation of society started to become apparent. Under such circumstances, every ten days the *Current Laws and Regulations* was first published and put out, starting from 3rd November 1950. Its aim was to explain state policy with priority given to the laws and regulations, and to be used as a supplementary reader to the *Official Gazette*. It is still published at present.

The *Commentary*, the supplement of the *Official Gazette*, in 1953 shows the beginnings of postwar government PR magazines. In fact, the independent publication of the *Photographic PR Information*, started in May 1954, was the very beginning. It was once called *The Graph-- Window of the Government*, and is now called *Photo*. The *Every-ten-days PR Information* also separated from the *Commentary*, the supplement to the *Official Gazette*, and was named the *Review-- Window of the Government* and is now called *Current Movement-- Window of the Government*.

As a result of the condition of printing and publishing at the Printing Bureau after 1946, there were only eight items published in 1946. Since then there have been large increases. The agreement "Concerning the Reinforcement of the Diffusion of

Government Publications" passed the Cabinet Council in November
1956. In 1956, 43 items were put out but the next year there
were 123 items. The total number of items published from 1946
up to 1966 amounts to 1,517. In 1966 there were 150 items and
as of August 1969, there were 180 items so far that year. The
total number of books and magazines on sale at the moment is
between 430 and 450 items.

The contents of the various books and magazines include politics, law, economics, finance, statistics, education, social
problems, natural sciences, engineering, industry, transport,
art and language. There are records such as the *Official
Gazette, Proceedings of the Lower House, Proceedings of the
Upper House* and *Statutes*, periodicals such as the *Laws and Regulations, Current Laws and Regulations* and *National Personnel
Authority Monthly* and annuals and non periodicals such as white
papers, statistics and reports.

NOTES:

1.   KONDO, Kanehiro, "Centralization of the Government
     Publications and the Printing Bureau", *Monthly
     Catalogue of Government Publications* 10:4, Tokyo,
     1966, p. 6.

2.   Printing Bureau of the Cabinet, *Brief History of
     the 50 Years of the Printing Bureau*, Tokyo, 1921,
     p. 29.

3.   —————, *History of the 70 Years of the Printing
     Bureau*, Tokyo, 1943, p. 204.

CHAPTER 2
DISTRIBUTION OF GOVERNMENT PUBLICATIONS

1.   The Structure of Government Publications
      Distribution

As seen, the production and publication process of government
publications is quite different from that of general publications. In utilizing government publications, the primary
requisite is to recognize uniqueness and to know the distribution method involved. Now let us look at the machinery of
the distribution.

Government publications in general have various purposes, they
can be for PR, reports, administrative purposes and records,
and are distributed according to the purpose. Distribution is
classified into two categories on the basis of subject. One is
group distribution, which is distribution for the organizations
concerned. The other is individual distribution for the
general public. When nothing is specified by the regulations,
each ministry and agency concerned decides on the method.

The organs of group distribution are the executive organs of
the national and local governments. The groups and bodies
concerned are as follows: research institutions, educational
institutions, public entities, libraries and establishments.
The method of group distribution is decided at the planning
level before the production of material begins. Therefore,
when the publications are ready, they are sent to groups according to the list. They are, as a rule, free of charge. As seen
previously, among the general materials of government publications there are three different types of publications, those
for sale, those not for sale and those sold at cost. The ones
not for sale, but sometimes sold at cost price and classified
as distribution for business, are for group distribution.
Distribution to libraries is prescribed by law. The Library
Law provides that "(1) the government shall offer libraries,

which are established by the metropolis and districts, two
copies each of the publications put out by the Printing Bureau
such as the *Official Gazette*, etc., that are utilized for PR
for the general public,(2) the national government and the local
public entities shall, complying with the request of the Public
Library, offer the publications put out by themselves and other
materials free of charge to the Public Library" (Article 9).
There are various interpretations as to whether they are free
or not. Megumu Nishizaki, for example, interprets it as follows:
"the purpose of this stipulation is to provide preferential
treatment to Public Libraries as regards official publications
with a view to utilizing them as PR information for the general
public. Especially in paragraph 1, they tried to stress this
because the libraries of urban and rural prefectures should be
the center of library services in the district. In paragraph
2, it is specified that they are free of charge, nevertheless,
in paragraph 1, it does not specify whether they are free or
not. It means that they can either be free or a charge made.[1]
Keijiro Inai states, "however, the government should make an
effort to provide them free of charge"[2].

Individual distribution is divided into (1) free distribution
to Diet members and (2) both free distribution and distribution
where a charge is made to the general public. In regard to the
former, it ought to be specified that they should be distributed
to each of the members, for instance, the Proceedings of Committees (Article 63 of the Lower House Regulations, and Article
58 of the Upper House Regulations). The documents which are
the concern of the Diet members are to be distributed to them.
They also make it a principle to offer the publication to those
concerned, although it is only distributed in compliance with
their request.

Each division of the ministry and agency that produces the
publication distributes free publications directly to the
general public. In some cases, however, according to the publication, the PR division of each organization takes care of it.
When a distribution plan is devised, priority is usually given
to groups that are more likely to make the most of the publication rather than to individuals. Therefore, the number of
these publications is inevitably limited. Moreover, the fact
is that each ministry and agency is unable to provide enough
publishing finance so they cannot publish many for the general
public. In any case, because the job of free distribution to
the public is left to each division of the ministry, there is
an infinite variety.

With respect to the "non-free" distribution of government publications, there are the following two kinds: one is published
by the Printing Bureau of the Ministry of Finance and sold at
the Service Center for Government Publications and Service
Stations while the other is published and sold by the body concerned or the commercial publishing company. The Service Center
for Government Publications and the Service Stations are the
sales agencies for government publications across the country,
that is, book stores especially for government publications.
Needless to say, they are also sold at leading book stores.
These Service Centers and Service Stations take the lead in the
government publication diffusion activity in the local districts.
At present, there are six national Service Centers for Government Publications established in Tokyo, Osaka, Nagoya, Fukuoka
and Sapporo. The privately-owned Service Centers for Government
Publications number 54, covering each seat of national and local
government throughout the nation.

Government publications put out by the body concerned or the
commercial publishing company are sold not only at the Service
Center and the Service Stations but also through distributors
at the retail book stores. But the users began to recognize
more and more that the Service Center for Government Publications, which was able to sweep away the old system and image
of the Sales Agency for the *Official Gazette*, deals with government publications. As a result, the Service Center for Government Publications and the Service Stations take a leading role
in distribution to the public.

2.   The Diffusion and Sales Organizations of
      Government Publications

HISTORY

The origin of the sales system of government publications in
Japan dates back to 1883 when the *Official Gazette* was established. At first the Post Bureau was in charge of sales, but
when the Official Gazette Bureau was established in 1885, it
took over the sales and set up the *Official Gazette* Sales Stand.
In 1889, they expanded their operations by establishing the
Sales and Distribution Agency for the *Official Gazette* in Kyoto
and Osaka. In 1899 it was named the Local Sales Agency for the
Official Gazette and was set up across the country. In regard
to the system, they repeatedly changed from direct sales to
consignment sales and vice versa up until 1921, when they finally

settled on the consignment system which is still used.

The diffusion mechanism for government publications based around
the Official Gazette sales had thus developed. With the out-
break and progress of the Pacific war and as the publishing
activity with a view to manipulating public opinion increased,
the Local Sales Agency for the *Official Gazette* was increased
and strengthened. By the end of 1941, there were about 6,800
Local Sales Agencies for the *Official Gazette* in the country.

In 1943 they numbered about 7,000. As they also dealt with
1.5 million copies of the *Weekly Review of Events* and 500,000
copies of the *Photograph Weekly*, the name was again changed to
the "Diffusion Department of the Official Gazette and the Weekly
in the Prefecture". After the war, in November 1945, as part
of the democratization under the GHQ it was renamed "Prefectural
Sales Agency for Government Publications", but by the next year
it was called "Prefectural Sales Agency for the *Official Gazette*".
Although they actively published books on social education, there
were only 813 agencies to deal with as of March 1948. As the
Official Gazette tended to decrease gradually, the Sales Agency
for it started to fail to come up to expectations for its development, because it was basically the sales organ for the *Official
Gazette*. Under such circumstances, there were indications of
some kind of a group organization on the basis of cooperation
and communication between the Sales Agencies themselves. In
November 1950 "The Association of the Local Sales Agency for the
Official Gazette" was finally established. With this association as its nucleus, "The Cooperative Association of the Local
Sales Agency for the *Official Gazette*" was started in April 1955,
which eventually marked a turning point for the postwar structure
of government publications sales system. In the following year
there was the Doubling of the *Official Gazette* Movement for a
year in response to the Printing Bureau of the Ministry of
Finance. It seemed to have achieved its purpose, as it met with
great response and recognition from the general public.

As life became stable, the people started to take greater
interest in government publications in order to learn the actual
conditions of, among other things, state politics, economics,
culture and education. At the same time the mass media had made
the most rapid progress, and this also meant greater demands for
government publications. However, at that time the sales system
was not mature and strong enough to meet such demands.

At about this time an English researcher on agriculture was

visiting Japan on an agricultural study, but he had no access
to the necessary government materials. He went to many places
such as the Printing Bureau and the Service Center for Official
Publications, which is the Service Center for Government Publications at present, and after visiting each department concerned
in the ministry and agency to seek the data he needed, his
efforts were in vain. He therefore composed a report containing
proposals and submitted it to each organization concerned and
the news agencies. It was almost the end of the year: 13th
December, 1955. His opinion appeared in a couple of leading
newspapers and some editorials took up this subject for discussion. He was Mr. R.P. Dore who was at the time a London
University Lecturer. He later revisited Japan, as one of the
five members of the OECD Educational Investigation Commission,
when he was a Professor at the University of Sussex. It is quite
ironic that the same idea as Mr. Dore's was raised inside the
Printing Bureau in 1927.

Originating from Mr. Dore's request, which indicated the weak-
ness of the distribution organization in Japan, and moreover,
as the time and the public also demanded, the government began
to discuss and examine this problem. Ishibashi, the then
Minister of International Trade and Industry, proposed as
follows: "we should study and consider establishing a sales
center where they deal extensively with government publications".
The plan for "Establishing the Sales Center for Government
Publications which makes an Exclusive Sale of the Publications
put out by each Ministry and Agency" was decided at the ordinary
Vice-Ministers Meeting, led by the speech that was made at the
Cabinet Council in September 1956. It was transferred to the
Prime Minister's Office, where they started to prepare a defi-
nite plan. The definite plan drawn up was based on the
following ideas: (1) to maintain and utilize the Government
Publications Center operated by the Printing Bureau, (2) to
start this three year plan around 1953, (3) to establish the
"Council for the Diffusion of Government Publications" in the
Prime Minister's Office with the "Service Center for Official
Publications" of the Cooperative Association of the Local Sales
Agency for the *Official Gazette*, which was founded in 1955, as
the central figure, (4) it should be composed of PR officials of
each ministry and agency, and (5) to utilize the Printing Bureau
for printing and publishing the Government publications. In
the original plan, however, it was stated that "the Printing
Bureau should execute printing and publishing", instead of
"to utilize the Printing Bureau for printing and publishing" by
which they aimed to establish the Anglo-American mechanism which

prints, publishes and sells as one organization. But in spite
of the latter expression, it is still not a centralized organization. In November 1956, the agreement "Concerning the
Reinforcement of the Diffusion of Government Publications" was
concluded.

"Concerning the Reinforcement for the Diffusion of Government
Publications"

(consented to by the Cabinet Council on 2nd November, 1956)

I.   Purpose

Although the books and other materials published by ministries
and agencies are extremely important for research and study on
various subjects and also are very valuable documents, they
have not been well used by the public.

Therefore, the acquisition of these official materials shall be
made easier for the general public, so that they will gain a
true appreciation of the conditions of national politics and
economics and so that the policies of the state will be absorbed
by the public.

Accordingly, concerning the material compiled by the government
which are to be sold or distributed (hereinafter referred to as
the Government Publications), the following means shall be
employed.

II.   Means

1.   Maintenance and Utilization of the Service Center for
      Government Publications.

In order to reinforce the diffusion of the Government publications still more, the present Service Stations shall be maintained and utilized. They shall not only display the government
publications intended for sale, but will also display and
distribute the government publications which are not intended
for sale, in cooperation with the ministries and agencies
concerned.

As the occasion arises, the same type of Service Center shall
be established in the metropolis to effect the diffusion of
Government publications.

2.   Publication of Government Publications

1.   The Council for the Diffusion of Government Publi-
     cations shall be established in the Prime Minister's
     Office, where they shall deliberate on the diffusion
     of Government Publications, such as the publication
     of Government publications and the management of the
     Service Center.

     The council shall be composed of the concerned
     ministry and agency officials.

2.   The ministry and agency shall collaborate in the
     reinforcement of the diffusion of government publi-
     cations, which are approved as the proper government
     publications for sale, by notifying the council
     in advance of the publications, and by submitting
     the Government publications and other materials which
     are not for sale to the council.

3.   The council shall, by contributing to the diffusion
     of government publications, compile the *Catalogue
     of Government Publications* (both monthly and
     annually).

4.   In regard to printing and publication, the ministry
     and agency shall utilize the Printing Bureau of the
     Ministry of Finance.

5.   For the smooth management of the council, the details
     of the management of the council shall be decided at
     the council meeting.

Note:

          The matter under consideration shall also apply to the
          legislature, the machinery of law, and other government
          related organs.

Based on this agreement, the Council for the Diffusion of Government Publications was inaugurated, and as the Regulations for
the Council (see Appendix 2) and the Items of Understanding
for the Council (see Appendix 3) were established, they went
into action. As the measures for the reinforcement of the
diffusion of government publications were taken, the Service

Center managed by the Printing Bureau and the Service Station,
which were actually the Sales Agencies for the *Official Gazette*
were set up and entrusted with the publications. They have
been producing excellent results through the sales organization
and promotion media. At the same time, for the convenience of
the users, they compile and publish the Catalogue of Government
Publications, which is a key to the sales of Government publications.

CURRENT CONDITIONS OF DIFFUSION AND SALES

Though the Council for the Diffusion of Government Publications
was inaugurated under legally disadvantageous circumstances,
i.e. the agreement by the Cabinet Council, it has been producing
excellent results due to the efforts of the parties concerned.
They gradually increased the number of Service Centers for
Government Publications managed by the Government, establishing
one in Tokyo in 1956, Osaka in 1959, Fukuoka and Nagoya in 1964
and Sapporo in 1965. At present there are six of them all
together throughout the country. In proportion to the increase
in the number of government publications displayed and as the
name "Service Center" becomes well-known, the total of users
increases. For example, the total number of users at the Tokyo
Service Center alone for the year 1957 was 40,750. In 1969 the
total at six centers across the country was 640,691. The figure
was an increase of 17 per cent over the previous year and users
per day exceeded 2,000. Let us look at the number of users at
each Service Center for the year of 1969. Kasumigaseki, Tokyo
had 253,649 annually and an average of 860 per day. Osaka
157,575; averaged 534 per day. Ohtemachi, Tokyo 74,080;
averaged 251 per day. Nagoya 67,923; averaged 230 per day.
Fukuoka 49,241; averaged 170 per day and Sapporo 34,124; 129.
In respect to the proceeds of sales, it is said that the figure
for 1967 is 31.3 times higher than that for 1957.

On the other hand, what the privately managed Service Station
for Government Publications was principally aiming at was, with
the six Service Centers across the country as their nucleus, to
form a network in each seat of the prefectural government and
to expand as much as possible. By 1963 they had established
32 Service Stations in 29 major cities and at present there are
54 Service Stations at each seat of the national and local
governments and other cities throughout the nation.

Besides these commissioned stores, appointed by the Printing

Bureau, there are some existing Local Sales Agencies for the *Official Gazette* where government publications are sold. As we have seen before, government publications are also sold at leading book stores, too.

As a part of the diffusion activity, they started the "Government Publications Diffusion Month" which lasted for a month from 27th October, 1967, in order to better acquaint the general public with government publications in connection with public bodies and private organizations. In 1969, this campaign was held for the third time. During the campaign, some books were displayed and some attractions put on at the six Service Centers and 54 Service Stations.

As for diffusion activity by private organizations, the "Exhibition on Government Publications" is held annually by the Council of Special Libraries. It is held in the library at the Chamber of Commerce and Industry, which is a member of the Council, and at the Administrative Documents Center in the prefecture. They exhibit government publications which were published in the previous year and receive a good response.

3.   Organizations that Collect and Offer Government
      Publications

OUTLINE

It is said that in regard to the distribution machinery each year, 25,000 books, including government publications, are put out and circulated. However, it is also said that usually only 30 per cent of them are displayed for sale at the retail book stores. R. Escarpit classified the demand for publications as follows: (1) fast-seller, which reaches its peak in about three weeks then its demand drops sharply, (2) steady-seller, which sells steadily for several years, and (3) best-seller type that begins with the fast-seller but ends with the steady-seller. As there are so many types of publications, there does not seem to be one certain formula, but, generally speaking, the demand is unlimited while the number of copies for the first edition is limited, therefore, if one misses the first publication one has to wait for a reprint. It is relatively difficult to acquire the materials needed even when it is a general book, although it is supposed to be comparatively easy to find out where, when and who published it. Consequently, when it comes to government publications, because it is so difficult to find

out the publisher, there is even greater inconvenience. Moreover, it is even more difficult to take advantage of the whole
collection of government publications, for they include quite
a few materials which are not-for-sale and materials designed
only for certain groups which do not circulate to the public.
Many of them are also serials. Therefore, when one studies
a certain subject, one would either have to acquire the whole
collection of desired materials, or rely on the organization
that collects these materials.

Accordingly, it would be necessary for one to become acquainted
with the organizations that collect government publications and
offer them for public use. Now let us observe the mechanism of
collection and supply of government publications.

DEPOSIT COPY SYSTEM IN JAPAN

The deposit copy system is a system which requires a publication
to be deposited with the state. It is supposed to be for the
control of publications and for the protection of the publishers.
In Japan it is regarded as a system similar to that of the Old
Publishing Law which tended towards strong control. However,
its purpose is now aimed at the protection of works and the
presentation of cultural inheritance rather than control and
censorship.

In most countries, the deposit copy of a publication is sent
to the National Library of that country. The deposit copy
system began in Japan in 1875. Under the provisions of the Old
Publishing Law, material was supposed to be deposited with the
Ministry of Home Affairs. At present, under the provisions of
the National Diet Library Law, it is to be deposited with the
National Diet Library. In the former deposit copy system,
based on the Old Publishing Law, the Ministry of Home Affairs
transferred all the deposited publications to the Imperial
Library, which was then the National Library and was once called
the Ueno Library, but is now called the National Diet Library.
The Old Publishing Law did not, however, specify the inclusion of
official documents within the category. In other words, Government publications were ignored by this system. But the Ueno
Library collected Government publications by depending on gifts
from the Government organizations. Owing to the success of the
international book exchange work of which the Ueno Library was
in charge, its collection was rewarded with good results.

At present, the deposit copy system is carried out in pursuance of Article 24 of the National Diet Library Law (9th February, 1948), which accepted the proposal concerning the deposit copy system of the state, expressed in the memorandum of the U.S. Library Mission.

It was partly amended on 6th June, 1949. In Article 24 paragraph 1, it is prescribed that "when the publications are published by or for various organizations of the state, they shall immediately deposit thirty copies if five hundred copies or more were published and less than thirty copies (depending on the decision made by the Librarian) if no more than five hundred copies were published, for the purpose of official use by the international exchange for other foreign Government publications and other international exchanges." Further they specify the number of deposits as follows: "when less than five hundred copies of a publication are published, unless otherwise specified, ten per cent of the publication shall be deposited."

The deposit copy of official documents, in regard to Article 24, was established on 9th September, 1948, as the National Diet Library made a request to each ministry and agency with the official note "Matter concerning the Deposit Copy of Publications of the State". Then each ministry and agency started to deposit their copies with the National Diet Library through their branch libraries.

Accordingly, at present the library in each ministry and agency is in charge of depositing their copies, and the National Diet Library transfers the deposited copy to the Public Libraries. However, Article 9 of the Library Law on the provision and collection of official publications, does not specify, as does the National Diet Library Law, the presentation of a deposit copy for the National Diet Library.

In addition to the deposit copy system of Article 24, these branch libraries are to submit thirty copies each for exchange between the ministries as a quasi-deposit copy under Article 17 of the National Diet Library Law. These thirty copies are to be exchanged among the thirty branch libraries in the administrative and judicial organs with an eye to improving the function of each library in the organ. Under Article 100 paragraph 12-15 of the Local Self-Government Law, it is stated that each local public entity should establish a local assembly library to which the Government supplies the *Official Gazette* and other Government publications. Under the provisions of the same

Article 100, the branch library in the national government organ is also obliged to deposit twenty copies for distribution to each of the libraries of municipal assemblies.

Furthermore, the Council of Special Libraries, founded in 1952, established the local council and the local materials center, where they provide a document service laying stress on Government publications. Since the branch libraries of Government organizations belong to the Council of Special Libraries, they distribute their official documents to these material centers. There are seven centers altogether, one in each district of the country.

Thus a total of 87 copies of any publication are deposited with the National Diet Library by the branch library, the library in the ministry and agency. These deposited copies are distributed to the other libraries and are used for international exchange.

In spite of the great efforts the branch library makes, the deposit copy system is not in fact satisfactory because of the following structural problems of the Government organizations.

1.   In the organization of the ministries and agencies there is, at the moment, no place where all government publications or a complete list of government publications are recorded.

2.   In each ministry and agency, no bureau or department receives all the publications, even their own.

3.   The publishing cost is a heavy expenditure for each ministry and agency. And as the budget is inadequate, the number of volumes they publish is restricted.

But, whatever the conditions may be, is it permissible for the state to disregard the very law that they stipulated?[3]   It is an important problem to be solved.

The thirty copies are maintained for preservation and for circulation, and some are distributed to 26 libraries of foreign countries by agreement, mostly national libraries. As mentioned before, international exchange in Japan can be traced back to 1875. The beginning was the exchange of publications between Japan and the U.S. The Ministry of Foreign Affairs was in charge of it up until May 1911, then the Imperial Library took charge when it was transferred to the Ministry of Education. Tsuyoshi Saito[4] gives the purpose of the international exchange

as follows: first, for the purpose of collecting materials, it
is to acquire foreign publications effectively and economically,
which are not available through the commercial route and, secondly, it is to deepen international understanding and eventually
contribute to intellectual cooperation and to peace and goodwill
in the world. Accordingly, this work of international exchange
is different from that conducted by an individual or a group,
because it is done by a special organization representing the
state. It is a very important project.

ORGANIZATIONS OFFERING SERVICES FOR GOVERNMENT
PUBLICATION USERS

It can be readily understood that libraries are also able to
offer some services in regard to government publications, as a
result of the collection and distribution structure. As well
as the Depository Library System in the U.S., a most distinguished one in the field, which we have seen already,
libraries in various countries offer many types of services.
In the U.S.A., the Public Document Library Division of the
Government Printing Office has the most comprehensive collection
of government publications. The Library of Congress also holds
a nearly complete collection of them. In England, though, there
is no depository library system as seen in the U.S., but they
have appointed the following five libraries as the Copyright
Libraries to which all the Government publications are deposited under law. They are the British Museum Library, the
National Library of Scotland, the National Library of Wales,
the Bodleian Library of Oxford University and the Cambridge
University Library. The Bodleian Library is especially well
known for its collection of government publications. Under
the law, these five libraries should receive government publications free of charge, but the university libraries in England
are obliged to purchase them. These libraries and university
libraries are to provide a system of services.

In our country the libraries do not have any particular system
or organization able to offer a systematic service as they do
in the U.S. and England. The libraries which collect, maintain
and make government publications available for utilization are
as follows: the National Diet Library, the branch library in
the administrative and judicial organs, the assembly library
of the municipal government, the Municipal Library, the library
in the Service Station for Government Publications, the University Library and the Materials Center of the Council of Special

Libraries. As far as the collections are concerned, all the
libraries but the National Diet Library are insufficient. This
must result at least in part from the operational problem of
the deposit copy and distribution system.

Supported by the deposit copy system from the Meiji era up to
the present, the National Diet Library comprehensively collects
and makes copies available to the users, this being its principal duty. The library in the ministries and agencies and the
branch library of the National Diet Library supplied not only
with their own publications but also many publications from
other ministries, can quite extensively collect and offer
services to the users.

The libraries of the municipal assembly receive from the
National Diet Library documents that were once submitted to the
National Diet Library, and utilize them for the user's aid.
The Municipal Assembly libraries are not furnished with sufficient materials but are still better than the Municipal
Libraries. Under the provision of Article 9 of the Library
Law, the Municipal Library is supposed to receive the distri-
butions, therefore, they should have a fairly good collection
of government publications. However, as regards the deposit
copy system, somehow the provision is not in this case as strong
as the Local Self-Government Law in the eyes of the law and as
a result they are not well organized and equipped. Naturally,
however, as it also depends on the attitude of the library, some
have an excellent collection and are capable of offering
excellent service.

The university libraries, too, are supplied with the materials
that concern them by each ministry and agency quite often. In
this case, the collection is usually more or less specific
rather than covering every subject.

The Materials Center of the Council of Special Libraries is a
promising library showing a gradual increase of the collections
supplied by the National Diet Library. It is also a unique
library because as the Materials Center for Government Publications, one center in each of the seven districts of Japan
provides services within the district.

The library of the Service Center for Government Publications
and the reading room of the PR division in each ministry and
agency have a collection mainly made up of current government
publications, but neither of them have adequate space. However,

the services that the PR division provides from the expert's point of view can never be surpassed, and it is an ideal aid.

That is the situation of various organizations today. Among them the National Diet Library and Materials Center of the Council of Special Libraries are prominent and are better equipped to discharge their duties. Accordingly, progress and improvement in this area can be expected.

NOTES:

1. NISHIZAKI, Megumu, *Library Law*, Tokyo, Haneda Shoten, 1950, p. 68.

2. INAI, Keijiro, *Explanation for Library Law*, Tokyo, Meiji Tosho, 1954, p. 56.

3. KUROKI, Tsutomu, "Collection and Proffer of the Government Publications", *Library World* 18:2, Tokyo, 1966, p. 59.

4. SAITO, Tsuyoshi, "History of the International Publications Exchange Program in Japan", (A series of Library Studies No. 5), Tokyo, National Diet Library, 1961, p. 166.

BIBLIOGRAPHY:

1. Printing Bureau of the Ministry of Finance, *History of the Printing Bureau of the Ministry of Finance*, Tokyo, 1962, 1,232 p.

2. KONDO, Kanehiro, "Centralization of Government Publications and the Printing Bureau No. 2", *Monthly Catalogue of Government Publications* 10:5, Tokyo, 1966.

3. SUGAI, Keiju, "Concerning the Reinforcement for the Diffusion of Government Publications", *Monthly Catalogue of Government Publications* 6:5, Tokyo, 1962.

4. MORI, Shigeru, "Concerning the Reinforcement Structure of Government Publications in the Printing Bureau", *Monthly Catalogue of Government Publications*

7:5, Tokyo, 1963.

5. SAKURAI, Yasunosuke, "Deposit Copy System of our
   Country", (A Series of Library Studies No. 5),
   Tokyo, National Diet Library.

6. OKADA, Narau, "Collection Policy and Collection of
   the Old Ueno Library" ibid.

7. YAMASHITA, Nobuyasu, "Deposit Copy System of the
   Government Publications" (A Series of Library
   Studies No. 14).

PART III

RETRIEVAL OF GOVERNMENT PUBLICATIONS

1. Method of Government Publications Retrieval

As we have seen so far, it is very hard to acquire or utilize
government publications quickly and efficiently because they
differ strikingly from regular publications in terms of the type,
number of publications, publishing organizations, and the method
of distribution. Government publications are one of the most
valuable information sources covering every area of human life.
However, obtaining data from Government publications puts a big
strain on researchers and other users.

From an economic viewpoint, one should spend little time in
retrieving the data. And for that purpose, some means and
methods which are faster and better are taken. For retrieval,
there are usually the following basic three steps of investigation (1) To find out if the publication that meets the purpose
exists or not, (2) if it does, where can it be found and if it
is available for one to acquire, and (3) to acquire or utilize
it. The publication catalogue, an index and bibliography of
government publications should be used as a tool for coping
with these investigations. In this sense, the catalogue, index
and bibliography are the key for data retrieval. Usually we
call them the secondary data. In other words, the secondary
data are the records in which they reorganized and reproduced
the primary data, the original materials. The secondary data
play a particularly important part in Government publications.

Kyosuke Arita, in his publication, *How to Collect Information*,
suggests that without any hesitation, one should ask the Government offices concerned for information[1]. This must be one of the
ways to acquire the desired information. The Public Relations
division is placed in each ministry and agency to answer inquir-
ies about materials, and if they do not handle the particular
subject, they introduce the inquirer to the department concerned.
This method may be too complicated and troublesome a way of
reaching the necessary data among such an enormous amount of
material. Nevertheless, Arita's idea reveals the truth that one
cannot utilize Government publications until one goes to the
Government organizations where they are produced.

Information and information data can be gained not only by the
secondary data method but also through personal contact, which
is always important. *The Handbook of Government Offices* compiled by the Prime Minister's Office and the annually published
Organization of the Government of Japan, compiled by the Administrative Management Agency, are very helpful in learning about

the organization of the government.

Tools such as the catalogue, index and bibliography, which help
us get to government publications, are classified into the
following three categories:

1. General Bibliography for Government Publications:
    the catalogue and bibliography of all the Govern-
    ment publications put out by the Government offices.

2. Bibliography for each Government Office: the cata-
    logue and bibliography that list all the publications
    put out by a certain organization of the Government.
    Some specific catalogues such as the subject cata-
    logue and the catalogue in foreign languages are
    included.

3. Trade Bibliography: basically a book list of the
    publications on sale and usually a catalogue of
    recent publications.

Depending on the purpose of the compilation and other circumstances, there are many types among the above-mentioned catalogues. Some are independently compiled and some are just one
part of a catalogue. There are monthly, quarterly and annual
catalogues and some are annotated while some are not.

As regards the history of the publication of the catalogue of
Government publications in Japan, as far as the general bibliography is concerned, there is no record for the period of the
Meiji and Taisho era. The beginning was the *Catalogue of Books
of the Government Organizations* which was founded in December
1927. This catalogue was compiled and published by the Printing
Bureau of the Cabinet. It was published quarterly, listing the
Government publications put out in the last three months. When
it was changed to a monthly catalogue in January 1938, they also
changed its name to the *Monthly Catalogue of Books of the Government Organizations*. In December 1943 when the war grew in
intensity, it was discontinued at volume 7, number 9. It was
a substantial work and a very useful catalogue of government
publications, as it was classified by government office and by
subject.

There have been several catalogues published after the war,
none of which was comprehensive. The only exception is the
Bibliography of the Government Publications, volume 1 to volume

8, 1945-1958. However, the catalogues of our country cannot
in general be compared with the exhaustive ones of the U.S. and
England, such as the *Monthly Catalog of United States Government Publications* and the *Government Publications Monthly List*
of England. Admitting the difficulty in this kind of work,
something must be done now to save the situation and to effect
a development. This should be an important task in the future
for the organizations concerned.

NOTES:
       1. ARITA, Kyosuke, *How to Collect Information*, Tokyo,
          Kobunsha, 1964, p. 34.

2.   General Bibliography for Government Publications

The General Bibliography for Government Publications, which
lists all the government publications in full, can also be
called the comprehensive catalogue. There are two types: one
compiled with legal support and another compiled independently.
As we have already seen the General Bibliography before the war,
let us now observe the ones after the war.

Under Article 7 of the National Diet Library Law, which prescribes that "the Librarian shall publish a catalogue or index
of the publications which are put out in Japan in the previous
year within a year's time", the *Deposit Copy Monthly* was founded
in October 1948 as a national bibliography. It was renamed the
Catalogue of Publications in Japan in July 1949 and was changed
again to the existing *Deposit Copy Weekly* on 18th June, 1955.
The *Japanese National Bibliography* is the accumulation of the
Deposit Copy Weekly and has been published annually in two
volumes since 1959. The Government publications are listed in
both of them as official publications classified by organization.
In 1959 and 1960 Government publications were collected in one
volume and published with the subtitle of "the Government
Offices". Therefore, except for these two cases, the independent
catalogue was not exclusively for government publications. But
as an inclusive catalogue, it can be used as a means of retrieval.

Next, the *Bibliography of the Government Publications* was
compiled and published. The National Diet Library started to
compile it by obtaining the cooperation of the branch libraries,
placed in each ministry and agency, with a view to making it
not only the general bibliography but also the Government

publications catalogue. The first volume of the collection of government publications, covering the period from September 1945 to the end of 1950, was published in 1952. After the volume of 1953, it was compiled and published until discontinued at volume eight of 1958, and thereafter it was superseded by the *Japanese National Bibliography*. This Union Catalogue is excellent and far superior to any other union catalogue in its exhaustiveness, and it is unfortunate that it ceased at the eighth volume.

Complying with the request, under the measure "Concerning the Reinforcement for the Diffusion of Government Publications", the *Catalogue of Government Publications* was established in January 1957. It was renamed the *Monthly Catalogue of Government Publications* and has been continued up to now as an annotated catalogue.

Besides these principal catalogues, the *Biblos* founded in 1950, compiled and published by the National Diet Library, began to list Government publications as the publications of the national government offices from the sixth volume of 1955.

As has been mentioned, all these union catalogues are incomplete. In regard to the Japanese National Bibliography, as long as the deposit copy system stays as it is we cannot hope for its improvement.

According to the author's survey on the *Japanese National Bibliography* and the catalogue published by each ministry and agency over the last ten years, the *Japanese National Bibliography* published only 70 to 80 per cent of government publications in proportion to the publication catalogues of their particular ministries. Moreover, these catalogues of the ministry and agency do not themselves contain all publications, and the figure should actually be lower.

As for the *Monthly Catalogue of Government Publications*, it is basically compiled from the reports of each ministry and agency that is submitted to the Office of Public Relations of the Prime Minister's Secretariat. It also cannot be exhaustive since the ministries and agencies do not obtain all of the materials, such as the inter-department documents. Besides, because it serves as the trade catalogue, it would be imagined that it is very hard to improve and develop its content.

As we have already looked at the current sources of weekly, monthly and annual catalogues, let us now look at the retro-

spective type of source catalogues, which are very few in number.
The only inclusive retrospective one is the *Exhibition of the
Official Publications - Catalogue and Explanation* compiled by
the National Diet Library and published in 1958. It is composed
of three parts: the first part lists the major Government publications in the early Meiji era, the second part, serving as the
comprehensive publications catalogue throughout the period,
continued the catalogue of publications which are classified
according to the different ministries and agencies, and the
third part listed the recent important Government publications.
There is also the *Catalogue of the Official Publications Exhibition* co-sponsored by the National Diet Library and the Council
of Special Libraries, which is still continued. It does not
collect as many publications as the *Exhibition of the Official
Publications - Catalogue and Explanation*, only collecting the
principal publications of the year.

For retrospective research, the Library Catalogue of the Ueno
Library, which is the National Diet Library at present and owns
a huge collection of Government publications after the Meiji
era, is a very useful source. The "Presentation of the Government Publications of Japan after the War" was published in the
Biblos (vol. 13-vol. 17) as an annotated bibliography, classified by each ministry and agency. This is also an excellent
source of data written by the specialists of each ministry and
agency.

NOTES:

> 1. KUROKI, Tsutomu, "A Study on Government Publi-
>   cations", *Annual of the Japan Society of Library
>   Science* 14:2, Tokyo, 1967, p. 20.

BIBLIOGRAPHY:

> 1. KIDERA, Seiichi, *Introduction to Library Materials*,
>   Tokyo, Meiji Shoin, 1969, 196 p.

3.   Bibliography for each Government Office

The Bibliography for each Government Office is the catalogue or
bibliography compiled or published by the Ministry and agency
for themselves. These catalogues and bibliographies are classified into two main groups, the publication catalogue and the

library catalogue. The former is a catalogue which lists the
publications of each ministry and agency. The latter is a
catalogue of the collection of the library in each ministry and
agency, including the news flash and the supplement catalogue.
Each publication catalogue and library catalogue contains both
current and retrospective types of sources.

With respect to the publication catalogue, it has been compiled
and published, though sporadically, for a long time. The *Publication List of the Ministry of Education* founded in 1884 and
the *Publication Book List of the Ministry of Agriculture and
Commerce* founded in 1899, are typical examples. This kind of
catalogue was actively published after the war. Some of the
principal publication catalogues which are sources of current
information include the *Publication Catalogue of the Ministry
of Education* and the *Publication Catalogue of the Ministry of
Finance*. The *Comprehensive Bibliography of Books* published by
the Ministry of Agriculture and Fishery in 1954 which covers
the period from 1945 to 1952 and the *Publication Catalogue of
the Ministry of Labour* published in 1950 covering 1947 to 1950,
are retrospective sources.

In many cases, the libraries where publications are collected
are in charge of compiling the catalogues. Some ministries have,
however, established a specific department or bureau which
controls the works and the publications. They are, the Textbook
Administration Division of the Ministry of Education, the Data
Processing Administration Division of the Ministry of International Trade and Industry, and the Management Division of the
Statistical Information Department in the Ministry of Agriculture
and Forestry. In the case of the Ministry of Agriculture and
Forestry, the Management Division serves as the publishing
bureau for the ministry. However, this is the only exception
and we cannot find this function elsewhere in the governmental
organizations.

The following are retrospective sources of publication catalogues
and bibliographies:

* *Publication Catalogue of the Executive Office of the National
  Personnel Authority*, as of 31st October, 1954, Library of
  Executive Office of the National Personnel Authority, 1955,
  18 p.

* *General Catalogue of the Materials Published* by the Statistics
  Bureau of the Prime Minister's Office, 1871 - February 1966,

Library of the Statistical Bureau of the Prime Minister's
Office, 1966, 116 p.

* *General Publication Catalogue of the Headquarters of the
  Economic Stabilization*, April 1949 - December 1950, Library
  of the Headquarters of the Economic Stabilization, 1951, 63 p.

* *ibid.*, January 1951 - December 1951, 1952, 77 p.

* *Publication Catalogue of the Ministry of Justice*, September
  1945 - December 1950, Law Library of the Ministry of Justice,
  1951, 53 p.

* *Publication List of the Ministry of Education*, as of 1884,
  Ministry of Education, 1884, 60 p.

* *Publication Catalogue of the Ministry of Education and Other
  Relating Organizations*, April 1950 - December 1950, Library
  of the Ministry of Education, 1951, 421 p.

* *Publication Book List of the Ministry of Agriculture and
  Commerce*, July 1881 - March 1899, Documents Department of the
  Ministry of Agriculture and Commerce, 1899, 86 p.

* *Publication Catalogue of the Ministry of Agriculture and
  Fishery*, as of 1948, Library of the Ministry of Agriculture
  and Fishery, 1949, 92 p.

* *Comprehensive Bibliography of the Books Published by the
  Ministry of Agriculture and Fishery*, September 1945 - December
  1952, Library of the Ministry of Agriculture and Fishery,
  1954, 239 p.

* *Publication Catalogue of the Maritime Safety Agency*, May 1948-
  October 1954, Library of the Ministry of Maritime Safety
  Agency, 1954, 13 p.

* *Publication Catalogue of the Ministry of Labour*, September
  1947 - June 1950, Library of the Ministry of Labour, 1950,
  37 p.

* *Publication Catalogue of the Ministry of Construction Classified by the Department and Bureau*, September 1945 - December
  1950, Library of the Ministry of Construction, 1951, 42 p.

The current publication catalogues are as follows:

* *Publication Catalogue of the Ministry of Finance*, from 1949 -
  , annually, Library of Ministry of Finance.

* *Publication Catalogue of the Ministry of Education*, from 1951-
  , annually, Ministry of Education.

* *Monthly Book List of the Ministry of Agriculture and Forestry*, from January 1950 -   , Library of the Ministry of Agriculture and Forestry.

* *Publication Catalogue of the Ministry of International Trade and Industry*, from 1953 -   , annually, the Ministry of International Trade and Industry (Appears in the *Material News Letter*).

The Library catalogue is compiled by the library of each ministry and agency and is the catalogue of the materials which are collected in their libraries. Accordingly, the library catalogue includes both the publications put out by themselves and the data and documents they collected for their job. It can be used as a first hand means of retrieval of Government publications. No ministry or agency fails to compile and publish this library catalogue. It should also be called the catalogue of holdings or the possession catalogue. In theory as these libraries inherited the book stock from pre-war institutions, their library catalogues are useful and used widely, but as far as the collection is concerned, some of the materials were lost in the period before the restoration of the new institutions.

It should also be noted that a remarkable source of information for data retrieval among government publications is not in the form of a catalogue but provides valuable up-to-date information, these being the columns which appear in the general PR materials of the PR division or in the individual PR materials and PR magazines put out by the departments concerned.

4.   Trade Bibliography

The trade bibliography is a catalogue for the purpose of sales. It could be included in the category of the General Bibliography. However, as their sales system is completely different from the commercial publishing company's Government publications rarely appear in the regular trade catalogue put out by the publishing company, much less in newspaper advertisements.

The trade bibliography is classified into two groups; one compiled and published by the sales agency for Government publications and the other compiled and published by the publishing organizations of the Government. Examples of the former are, the *Monthly Catalogue of Government Publications* compiled by the Council for the Diffusion of Government Publications, the *Annual Catalogue of the Government Publications and Other*

Materials compiled by the Cooperative Association of the Local
Sales Agency for the *Official Gazette*, and the *Government
Publications Newspaper* by the same association.

As we have seen, the *Monthly Catalogue of Government Publications* is compiled in accordance with the agreement "Concerning
the Reinforcement for the Diffusion of Government Publications"
of the Cabinet Council. The first series of the first volume
of the *Monthly Catalogue* was published in January 1957 collecting
Government publications put out during the period from January
to December 1956. From the second series of the first volume,
it was compiled on a monthly basis and named the *Monthly Catalogue* continuing to the present. It is classified with reference
to periodicals and non-periodicals with an annotation for each
entry. It is compiled with the materials and publications
reports and presented, by each ministry and agency, to the chairman of the council, the Director of the Office of Public
Relations of the Prime Minister's Office, by the first day of
the month. They make it a rule to also publish the not-for-
sale items.

It was started because of the increasing demand and interest in
sales of Government publications. In a way, it succeeded the
traditional pre-war publication, the *Monthly Catalogue of Books
of the Government Organizations*, but the difference, due to the
change in organization of the Government and its operations,
between the former and the latter is the number of publications
collected in it. In other words, the pre-war publication
exceeds the current one in the number of items carried in it.
They are, however, making efforts to improve it, because it is
the only one of the kind.

The *Annual Catalogue of Government Publications and Other
Materials* is compiled for sale at the Service Center for Government Publications and the Local Sales Agency for the *Official
Gazette*. It is classified into six subjects, such as white
paper, yearbook, annual reports, investigation reports of actual
conditions, Statute books, etc. It is very convenient because
it lists publications on the same subject in one place.

The *Government Publications Newspaper* is published by the Cooperative Association of the Local Sales Agency for the *Official
Gazette*. It receives and introduces Government publications.
It was established on 5th March, 1968 and is now published on
the fifth and twentieth days of the month. Actually they had
revived the publication of the former *Government Publications*

Newspaper, which was founded on 10th June, 1964 and was published once a month until 10th September, 1966. At any rate, it has a substantial content and is unique.

The trade bibliographies put out by the publishing organizations for Government publications are as follows: the *Monthly Catalogue for Government Publications of the Printing Bureau of the Ministry of Finance*, and *Publication Catalogue of the Printing Bureau of the Ministry of Finance*, both of which are put out by the Printing Bureau, the *General Catalogue of Government Publications and Others* which is compiled and published by the Liaison Committee of the Diffusion of Government Publications, and some others put out by commercial publishing companies.

The former two are catalogues collecting government publications put out by the Printing Bureau, the central printing office and the publishing organization of the Government. The *Monthly Catalogue* prints publications put out during the previous month, and the *Publication Catalogue* collates the publications for sale and is put out biannually. The *Publication Catalogue* is classified by the following subjects: social science, natural science, engineering, industry, art, languages and periodicals, and is also annotated.

The *General Catalogue of Government Publications and Others* was founded in 1970 and is put out annually. As the title implies, it includes about 2,000 items of special technical books on administration and other areas relating to the Government besides genuine Government publications. It is classified by ministry and agency and subdivided into the following categories; laws and regulations, statistics and commentary with short annotations.

The trade catalogue of a publishing company is their regular trade catalogue which collects both the government publications and other publications being put out.

PART IV

ANNOTATIONS OF GOVERNMENT PUBLICATIONS

INTRODUCTORY REMARKS

1. Coverage of collection

   a. The publications listed in this book are those books or
      periodicals published until December 1977, which are
      regarded as basic data or information.

   b. They include general informative materials such as those
      from periodicals, research, statistics, reports and
      white papers. Emphasis is placed on basic materials
      which have been and will be regularly published.

2. Order of listing

   The List is classified in the following three groups:

   (1) Periodicals

   (2) White Paper

   (3) Investigations, Statistics, Reports, etc.

   The order of publications listed is according to the order
   of Governmental agencies as shown in the *Administrative
   Structure Chart* of 1977, by the Administrative Management
   Agency. The names of the Governmental agencies are based
   on the *Organization of the Government of Japan*, English
   edition, 1977, by The Agency.

3. Annotation

   An objective explanation as to the content of each publication is made, considering that it will serve as a fundamental source of information.

4. Form of entry

   Each publication is introduced in the order of: Editing
   agency, title (Japanese title), volume and number, year of
   foundation, frequency, publisher. In the case of a publication which has a sub-title, it is indicated right after
   the title with a "_", a serial publication is indicated by
   a short line "-" following the time of foundation. The
   editing agency is identified by the section of a particular
   bureau or department. The publisher is identified as the
   company or individual selling the publication.

CHAPTER 1
PERIODICALS

The Cabinet Secretariat, The Cabinet Research Office.
   A Research Monthly Report (Chosa Geppo) No. 1 - January
   1956 - Monthly Printing Bureau, Ministry of Finance

A collection of research and studies on the situations here and
abroad. Articles included are the results of work done within
the Office and they do not in any way reflect the official view
of the Cabinet.

The main purpose of this publication is to provide reference
material for researchers in the Cabinet, and governmental and
other parties concerned, therefore editorial emphasis is placed
on articles, informative materials in foreign countries and
diaries of important problems.

National Personnel Authority, Bureau of Administrative Services,
   Administrative Section.
   National Personnel Authority Monthly Report (Jinjiin Geppo)
   May 1950 - Monthly Printing Bureau, Ministry of Finance

This was initially issued by the Information Bureau of the
National Personnel Authority to publicize the work of the
Authority, but later turned out to be a comprehensive magazine
on personnel administration and the problems of Government
workers.

Various personnel administrative questions are dealt with in
the form of commentaries, lectures, round-table talks and so
forth.

Information on personnel administration in other countries,
recommended changes in system and notification are also included.

Minister's Secretariat, Prime Minister's Office, Office of
Public Relations.
    Photo (Photo) May 1954 - Fortnightly   Jijigaho-sha
    Publishing Co.

A popular information magazine initially started as *Photo
Official News* in May 1954. The title was changed to *Graph -
the Window of the Government* in May 1960, and finally to *Photo*
in May 1961.

Information available on the Government is shown by photographic
means in order to achieve greater public understanding of
Government policies. It can be described as an "easy to understand" graphic magazine.

It also serves as an introduction to various countries of the
world as well as for many parts of Japan. At the moment it is
not intended to be for propaganda purposes.

Prime Minister's Office, Minister's Secretariat, Office of
Public Relations.
    Current Movement (Tokino Ugoki) May 1957 - Fortnightly
    Printing Bureau, Ministry of Finance

A Government information magazine initially started under the
title of *Official Bulletin* and published every 10 days. It
later became the *Commentary - Window of the Government* (1st
July, 1960).

A booklet to explain governmental policies in an easy manner in
order to achieve wider public understanding. Each issue features
one Ministry with a detailed explanation. Besides feature
articles, regular items such as round-table talks, commentaries,
serial articles and other informative materials are included.

Prime Minister's Office, Minister's Secretariat, Office of
Public Relations.
    Monthly Public Poll (Gekkan Seron Chosa) June 1969 -
    Monthly Printing Bureau, Ministry of Finance

Increasing numbers of public polls have been conducted by both
Governmental and private agencies. As a result they found the
necessity for material giving a comprehensive picture of the
trends of public opinion. This magazine came to be published

in response to that demand.

Each issue reports the outcome of a public poll carried out in the month of issue, and an outline of nation-wide surveys conducted by both those of the public and private sectors.

Administrative Management Agency, Inspection Division.
    Monthly Report of Administrative Inspection (Gyosei
    Kansatsu Geppo) No. 1- October 1959 - Monthly

This is a monthly report replacing the *Administration Inspection Annual* published from 1953-1959, to publicize the work carried out by the Inspection Division to agencies concerned and the public at large.

Information includes: Inspections of National and Local Plans and the current situation of the administration.

Economic Planning Agency, Research Bureau, Domestic Research Section.
    Economy Monthly Report (Keizai Geppo) October 1947 - Monthly
    Economic Planning Association

This is a report providing analysis on economic trends based on statistical data with the following contents: analytic outlines of prices, finance and financing, international balance of payments, mining industry production, enterprises, labour, and life of the people.

Recent issues also include future perspectives of economy and management.

Economic Planning Agency, Research Bureau, Statistics Section.
    Japan Economy Indicator (Nippon Keizai Shihyo) October 1951-
    Monthly Printing Bureau, Ministry of Finance

This is a compilation of useful statistical data for looking into industrial fluctuation, and major economic data necessary for analysis of economic trends. Particularly, major economic data covering the latest information under the classification of industrial activities, international trade and balance of payments, financing, national products, and outcome of predicted researches.

Editing of this magazine is done in collaboration with the
Legislation Reference Bureau of the National Diet Library.

Scientific Technology Agency.
   Monthly Report of Scientific Technology Agency (Kagaku
   Gijutui Cho Geppo) September 1956 - Monthly Printing
   Bureau, Ministry of Finance

A magazine aiming to publicize the work of the Agency, as published on the first of each month. Contents include important
policies, budget concerns, promotion of scientific research,
introduction to scientific technology, statistical data, outlines of attached institutions, and activities of various
councils within the Agency's framework.

Atomic Energy Bureau, Science and Technology Agency.
   Atomic Energy Commission Monthly Report (Genshiryoku Iinkai
   Geppo) May 1956 - Monthly

Summarized reports of development and utilization of atomic
energy. Articles therefore include the background materials
and minutes of Atomic Energy Commission Meetings, in addition
to resolutions adopted, and reports of activities of the Atomic
Energy Bureau.

A good guide to the progress of the Commission and at the same
time a magazine suitable for the general public.

Ministry of Foreign Affairs, International Information Bureau,
Research Section.
   Ministry of Foreign Affairs Researches Monthly Report
   (Gaimusho Chosa Geppo)
   Vol. 1 No. 1- 1960 - Monthly

Publication of research activities made by the Ministry of
Foreign Affairs. Articles collected are views of writers and
do not reflect the official views of the Ministry. The Ministry
dispatches a certain number of research attachés to embassies
all over the world.

This magazine includes research made through this information
network and sometimes research made by Embassy personnel
themselves.

Ministry of Foreign Affairs, Economic Affairs Bureau.
    Economy and Diplomacy (Keizai to Gaiko) January 1951 -
    Fortnightly   Economic Diplomacy Study Group

This is a collection of comments and papers produced by
interested sections within the Ministry centred on the Economic
Affairs Bureau and the Economic Diplomacy Study Group composed
of representatives of trading companies.

The economy in relation to diplomacy, and vice-versa, are
compiled from an international viewpoint.

Occasionally there are some featured topics and it generally
includes commentaries and reports of current trends in economics and diplomacy here and abroad, reports of international
conferences, and reports of negotiations. As an appendix,
Release on Economic Trends by Embassies and Consulates are
distributed to the subscribers.

Ministry of Finance, Minister's Secretariat, Correspondence
Section.
    Finance - Publicity of Ministry of Finance (Finance -
    Okunasho Koho) December 1965 - Monthly   Financial Affairs
    Association

This is a PR magazine of the journal type. Commentaries on
financial and economic tendencies, activities of respective
research and study institutes and councils, Ministerial
announcements, ordinances, briefs released on Parliamentary
discussions, important events, and press-release information
are compiled so that the activities of the Ministry could be
understood at a glance.

Ministry of Education, Minister's Secretariat, Research Section.
    The Monthly Journal of the Ministry of Education (Monbu
    Jiho) No. 1 - May 1920 - Monthly   Gyosei Ltd., Publishing
    Co.

A review with a long history continuously published since 1920.
Occasionally published during the initial period. The editing
agency altered from time to time due to structural changes
made within the Ministry, for its issues No. 1 to No. 823 in
1945. Regularly published since its issue of No. 824 in
January 1946. During this period, the major contents covered

Legislation, notifications, announcements, commentaries, and the
review had the nature of an administrative resource book. Since
its issue No. 824, its editing policy changed to that of an
educational magazine, compiled by the Ministry.

Presently included are: explanations of educational legislation,
information on education, introduction on education of other
countries, and comments on educational problems.

Ministry of Education, Minister's Secretariat, Statistics
Section.
        Statistics and Education (Tokei to Kyoiku) No. 1 December
        1950 - Bi-monthly DAI-ICHI HOKI Publishing Co., Ltd.

Originally named *Kyoiku Tokei Geppo* (Monthly report of Educational Statistics). The title changed to *Educational Statistics* after issue No. 6, when the frequency of the publication
became bi-monthly. Finally changed to its present title from
issue No. 101.

Statistics on education and culture based on statistical theories
and methods, educational statistics, and education in statistics
at school are at the centre of the coverage provided by this
magazine. Articles are compiled under headings of Commentary,
Course and Explanation.

Ministry of Education, Primary and Secondary Education Bureau,
Primary Education Section.
        Primary Education Information (Shotokyoiku Shiryo) May
        1950 - Monthly TOYOKAN Publishing Co., Ltd.

This is a magazine dealing with a wide-range of problems in
primary education. Management of schools as well as classes,
the contents of courses and teaching subjects are covered.
Having the form of "featured topics" each issue contains some
articles and essays under headings of commentary, study
materials, actual cases of teaching, and current news. Occasionally, reports from various study meetings are made. In case of
revision of guidelines a special issue is published.

Ministry of Education, Elementary and Secondary Education
Bureau, Secondary Education Section.
        Secondary Education Material (Chuto Kyoiku Shiryo)

January 1952 - Monthly DAINIPPON TOSHO Publishing Co., Ltd.

This is a magazine dealing with important problems involved in secondary education. Policies of the Ministry and commentaries of experts are covered. Each issue has a featured topic, and under the topic, commentaries, explanations, cases of teaching and trends in secondary education are compiled. A special issue usually provides the latest announcements in case of revisions of guidelines.

Ministry of Education, Primary and Secondary Education Bureau, Vocational Education Section.
     Industrial Education (Sangyo Kyoiku) June 1951 -
     Monthly Employment (Problems) Study Institute

A magazine taking advantage of the enactment of the Industrial Education Promotion Act in June 1951, with the aim of contributing to the promotion of industrial education.

Articles compiled are contributed by those interested in business, academic and educational fields. Also included are commentaries on industrial education, explanation on subjects, and information from the Vocational Education Section.

Ministry of Education, Primary and Secondary Education Bureau, Local Affairs Division.
     Monthly Report of Education (Kyoiku Iinkai Geppo) July
     1949 - Monthly DAIICHI HOKI SHUPPAN Publishing Co., Ltd.

This is a liaison-oriented magazine first published at the commencement of the Board of Education system in 1948, which played an important role until the newly adopted system became established.

Problems centred on educational administration on both the national and prefectural levels. Contents include explanation of laws, the situation of prefectures, and current educational topics.

Ministry of Health and Welfare, Minister's Secretariat, Statistics and Information Department.
     Monthly Business Report of Social Welfare Administration
     (Shakai Fukushi Gyosei Geppo) Vol.1 No.1 - January 1951 -
     Monthly

It was formerly the *Social Welfare Statistical Monthly* until
volume 12, when the title changed to the present one. This
Monthly serves as a quick release on various data, which later
will be included in the *Annual Report of the Social Welfare
Administration*. Data dealt with is classified into: Life
protection, protection of women, protection of children, welfare
commissioners, etc. A quarterly review and a half-a-year review
are also compiled.

Ministry of Health and Welfare, Minister's Secretariat, General
Affairs Section.
    Health and Welfare (Kosei) Vol. 1. No. 1 - April 1949 -
    Monthly Welfare Study Institute

Published following *Welfare Publicity Bulletin* (KOSEI KOHO
DAYORI), it is a journal covering the administration of social
welfare and other items centred on welfare.

It is a comprehensive journal dealing also with the problems of
workers in the field in addition to those of the national administration - compiled mainly under the headings of explanation
of welfare legislation, comments by experts, comments from local
workers, and topics from home and abroad, etc.

Food Agency, Administration Department, Administration Division.
    Food Information (Shokuryo Koho) Vol. 1 No. 1 - March
    1951 - published every ten days. RYOYO SHA Publishing Co.,
    Ltd.

An information bulletin providing government ordinances,
announcements, public information, notifications and the names
of magazines necessary for the staff members concerned.

It also has a publicity purpose for the public at large.

Ministry of International Trade and Industry, Minister's
Secretariat, Research and Statistics Department.
    Trade and Industry Statistics (Tsusan Tokei) January 1948 -
    Monthly Trade and Industry Research Association

It started under the title of *Monthly Report of Commerce and
Industry* in January 1943. The title changed to *Monthly Report
of Trade and Industry* in November 1949, and finally to the

present title in April 1963.

It provides a means of quick release of statistics held by the
department, covering articles under the heading of analysis of
recent surveys and statistics, production tendencies and statistical resource materials.

The Patent Office, General Administration Department, Publication
Division.
    Official Reports on Patents (Tokkyo Koho) 1888 - Daily
    Invention Association

An announcement of patents obtained is made in this report based
on the Public Announcement system. One has to apply to the
Patent Office to get patents for a new invention, submitting
together with the title and other particulars.

After some changes since the Meiji Era, the system of making
public announcements was firmly established in 1921 by this
official report, and this has been followed until today. As the
law prescribes, some reports are published according to classification.

The frequency of publication of these reports varies from daily
Patent Official Report, bi-weekly *Utility Model Patent Report*,
and *Design Report* to weekly *Trademark Report*.

Ministry of Transport, Minister's Secretariat, Correspondence
Section.
    Transport (Unyu) Vol. 1 No. 1 - June 1951 - Monthly
    Transport Association (Unyu koshi kosei kyokai)

A journal to explain the administration of transportation in
general. Commentaries, outline and explanation of the policies,
reports of current problems arising in land transportation,
marine transportation and air transportation, and tourism, by
responsible sections and concerned enterprises, are covered.

Ministry of Posts and Telecommunications, Radio Regulatory
Bureau.
    Radio Wave Review (Denpa Jiho) Vol. 1 No. 1 - April 1946 -
    Monthly Radio Wave Promotion Association

This is a magazine originally published under the name of the
Radio Wave Bulletin (Denpa Iho) in 1946, by the Ministry of
Postal Services centering on the radio. Explanation of regulations, commentaries, trends both inside and outside the
country, technological development and its practical utilization
in the field of radio are included.

It is a useful reference tool in order to know the legislation,
revision of laws, and other developments after WWII. An index
according to the main subject of articles which appeared from
the issue of May 1948 to the one of December 1969 is made in
Vol. 25 July issue by Mr. Uchimasa Sakogaki in his article *How
to make use of Radio Wave Review*.

Ministry of Labour, Minister's Secretariat, General Affairs
Division.
    Labour Review (Rodo Jiho) March 1948 – Monthly Labour
    Legislation Association

This is a bulletin as well as publicity magazine of the Ministry
of Labour on labour administration and labour problems in
general. It is not only an analysis of labour relations within
the country, but an analysis of research on trends in other
countries.

In addition, an outline of the administration and policies,
reports of round-table talks and current news are also included.
References include the Ministry's ordinances and legislations.

Ministry of Labour, Labour Standards Bureau.
    Labour Standards (Rodo Kijun) April 1948 – Monthly
    Japan Labour Study Institution

A PR magazine in which administration of labour standards,
current topics of industrial safety, personnel management,
industrial sanitation, wages management, etc. are taken up and
explained. It occasionally contains "featured topics", current
news, "personnel management consultation" useful for those
responsible for the job, statistical data, and an introduction
of reference books is generally included to provide a wide-range
of information.

Ministry of Construction, Minister's Secretariat, Information

Office.
   Construction Monthly (Kensetsu Geppo) January 1948 - Monthly
   Construction Information Council

This is a PR magazine on construction administration. Explanations and comments on policies of National Land Planning,
Road, River, Housing and City Planning are made. Articles are
classified under such headings as: Construction Review,
Priority Policy, study reports, current trends of construction,
major construction index.

Ministry of Home Affairs, Study Institute in Administrative
Division.
   Local Autonomy System. Local autonomy (Chiho Jichi) No. 1 -
   September 1947 - Monthly GYOSEI, Ltd.

This is a magazine concerned with the introduction of newly
enacted acts and reports of current problems of local governments. It also provides information on recent movements in
local governments.

Practical reference materials are given in a serial article
titled "Questions and Answers on Local Autonomy Legislation -
article by article", and "reference" in which Legislation
materials are recorded.

Ministry of Home Affairs, Administrative Bureau, First Public
Servant Division.
   Monthly of Local Government Workers (Chiho Komuin Geppo)
   No. 1 March 1953 - Monthly DAI ICHI HOKI SHUPPAN

A magazine aimed at promoting a better liaison between central
and local government, dealing with the local public servant
system in general. Contents include, laws explanation of the
system, commentaries on the public servant system in general,
practical business, and statistical data on current tendencies.

The National Diet Library, Research and Legislation Reference
Department.
   Reference (REFERENCE) May 1951 - Monthly

Quick release of the work done by the Research and Legislation
Reference Department of the National Diet Library. Its contents

cover the wide fields of politics, economy, society, education, and provides first-hand information in those fields in other countries. Articles are classified as "Research studies", "reference material", and "Quick Release".

The National Diet Library, General Affairs Department.
    Monthly Report of National Diet Library (Kokuritsu Kokkai
    Toshokan Geppo) April 1961 - Monthly   YURINDO

A magazine issued in place of the *Official Report of National Diet Library* which had been published from January 1949 to March 1961. Although it is a public magazine, it does not aim to publicize National Diet Library policy, and it largely consists of articles dealing with problems peculiar to the library.

Features include such columns as "Books not on sale in the book-store" which introduces materials of interest collected from among books obtained through international exchanges and contributions within the country.

The column of "reference" in this sense is regarded as excellent.

CHAPTER 2
WHITE PAPER

Prime Minister's Office, Central Council on Juvenile Problems.
    White Paper on Youth - Actual situation on Youth Problems
    and Countermeasures (Seishonen Hakusho) 1956 - Annual

This is a White Paper, principally to present to the general
public the basic facts and the actual situation of youth problems
and Government counter-measures. Questions on youth are discussed from such aspects as: Health and Welfare, Education,
Labour, Social Environment, Juvenile Delinquency based on
materials prepared by the government agencies concerned.

Emphasis in editing, however, has been changing to "Analysis of
the Actual Situation of youth and the Government's policy on
youth". The issue for 1968 devotes some pages to reviewing the
youth problems in the preceding decade.

At the end of each issue, the government budget on youth, and
the activities of the Central Council of Youth Problems are
reproduced. This paper was initially entitled the White Paper
on *Youth and the Child*, later the title was changed to the
present one.

Prime Minister's Office
    Annual Report on Tourism (Kanko no Jyokyo ni Kansuru Nenji
    Hokoku) 1963 - Annual

This is generally called the *Tourism White Paper*. Although the
WHITE PAPER is a term used for the publication of a report to
the Diet, this particular paper includes Tourism policy projected
for the following year.

Based on Article 5 of the Fundamental Tourism Act, this White

Paper is published exactly as reported to the Diet session.
The paper consists of 3 parts: Part I General - analysis of
tourism tendencies inside and outside Japan; Part II - situation
of tourism and policies toward tourism; Part III - tourism
policy projected for the following year. In Part II, an analysis
of people's life, and the transition of working hours is made
and based on this background information, the quantity of tourism, and changes in the form of travel are compared. With
regard to international tourism, the number of foreign travellers, Japanese travellers going abroad, and the balance of
payments of international tourism are clarified.

Reference is also made to the control of such tourist resources
as natural parks, hot spas, forests, cultural treasures, and
other facilities.

Part III announces the policy to be taken in the next year in
regard to the actual situation.

Fair Trade Commission

　　　Annual Report of Fair Trade Commission (Kosei Torihiki
　　　Iinkai Nenji Hokoku) 1947 - Annual

This is a report submitted to the Diet according to Article 44
sub-clause (1) regarding the Prohibition of Private Monopoly
and ensurance of fair trade, by the Fair Trade Commission every
year. It is generally called the *Monopoly White Paper*.

There is an annual report of the activities and achievements of
the Commission in the protection of the interests of the consumer and in the prohibition of unfair trade and the promotion
of the sound development of the Japanese economy.

Activities included are: Stock holdings and incorporation of
companies, permission of joint action, business concerned with
prevention of postponement of payment to subcontracts etc.
business concerned with the prevention of unreasonable premiums
and unfair indications (of quality, quantity, and price), survey
of production concentration of major enterprises, juridical
reports concerning the Anti-monopoly Law.

Economic Planning Agency
　　　Annual Economic Report (Nenji Keisai Hokokusho) 1947 - Annual

This is commonly called the *White Paper on the Economy* issued by the Economy Stabilization Bureau. The *Report on Economics Actual Facts* was the first White Paper ever published.

The Economic Planning Agency has been contributing through its economic policies to the economy of the country, including a 5-year Economic Development Plan for 1967-71 which started right after the termination of the medium-term economy plan. This paper is intended to report to the general public the general situation of the Japanese economy and its problems and also the future direction.

The paper consists of two parts, the first part is devoted to an analysis of the economic trends of the year. The second part is devoted to observation and suggestions for the future of the Japanese economy based on the present situation and long-term predictions.

Since 1968, two reports have been published for readers, convenience; one being "general" and the other "general and additional reference materials".

Economic Planning Agency

   Annual Review of the World Economy (Nenje Sekai Keizai Hokoku) 1959 - Annual

This is commonly called the *World Economic White Paper*, outlining the tendencies and major problems in the world economy for the year and is published annually at the end of the fiscal year.

The tendencies in the world economy of the year are outlined, followed by an analysis of the change in world economic structure and finally by clarification of factors for foreseen changes in the world economy.

The Analysis of the tendencies of the world economy is based on statistical data from various governments, the OECD, the IMF and research conducted by the Economic Planning Agency.

This report, with the analysis made by the Agency on the world economic tendencies provides good reference material in order to understand the status of the Japanese economy in the world.

Economic Planning Agency
    White Paper on People's Livelihood (Kokumin Seikatsu
    Hakusho) 1956 - Annual

The *Basic Findings of Changes in People's Living Standards* was
published in 1956 to make clear how the people were living.
This was the first White Paper on the subject. Subsequent
issues had sub-titles, under which changes in living standards
were analyzed comprehensively.

Consequently, the content varies from year to year, but each
issue looks at the life of the public at large in the previous
year, and identifies the problems in every aspect of life. An
analysis of life is made from three viewpoints: household
economics, movements in consumer prices, and the social aspect.
Identification of problems is limited to indication only. In
the 1969 issue a living standard index was made and the Japanese people's living conditions were compared with those of
European countries, in order to provide a guideline and a goal
for improving living standards.

Science and Technology Agency

    White Paper on Science and Technology (Kagaku Gijutsu
    Hakusho) 1958 - Irregular

Having been published in 1958 for the first time, a second issue
was published in 1962; subsequently, this White Paper has been
annually published.

The paper is meant for reporting and publicizing the general
situation of scientific technology, in particular research
activities and their problems, and suggestions for future policies to promote science and technology.

Each issue has subtitles such as "Situation of Science and
Technology in Japan" (1967), "Promotion of Self-help Development
of Technology" (1968) etc. Every issue contains general
descriptions and the role of scientific technology, governmental
policies, and detailed expositions as to research in the development of atomic energy, space, the oceans, pollution - preventive
technology, information techniques, biological techniques, etc.

Science and Technology Agency
   Atomic Energy Annual Report (Genshiryoku Nenpo) 1956 –
   Annual

This is generally called the *Atomic Power White Paper*, reporting
the trend in Atomic Power development and its exploitation in
Japan by the Atomic Energy Commission. General remarks and
detailed expositions are made separately, the former covering
an outline of the peaceful use of atomic energy, and the latter
covering the development of atomic power-operated furnaces,
atomic power generation, nuclear fuel, atomic ships, exploitation
of radio active rays, basic studies, safety measures, international cooperation, the training of technicians and expertise
in the atomic field, etc.

Having the form of an annual report, editorial policy (as seen
in the sub-title "trends and indications of new dimensions") is
based on efforts to cope with new developments in the situation.

Research Institute of Ministry of Justice
   White Paper on Crime (Hanzai Hakusho) 1960 – Annual

White Paper on Crime was a sub-title of the *Crime and its
Counter-measures in Japan*, published for the first time in 1960.
From the second issue, however, the White Paper became the main
title having a sub-title each year. Violence and juvenile
crime have been used as sub-titles for some years, and "Crime
and the Treatment of Criminals" has been the sub-title for
recent issues.

This White Paper describes the recent situation as regards crime
and countermeasures taken by the government. Outline of crimes
committed during the year, detailed description by types of
crimes, and treatment of the criminals form the content. Detailed expositions making full use of the latest data of the
Metropolitan Police Board provide valuable reference materials
for the consideration of countermeasures.

Ministry of Foreign Affairs
   Recent Situation of Japan's Diplomacy (Waga Gaiko no Kinkyo)
   No. 1 1957 – Annual

This is commonly known as the Blue Paper on Diplomacy, focussing
on major movements and the actual situation of diplomatic

policies taken in the year of issue.

Unlike a White Paper which points out problems in policies and
actions in addition to reporting the activities, this Blue Paper
describes only facts on the activities of the Ministry of Foreign
Affairs, eventually becoming "a record of activities".

The Blue Paper is so compiled as to explain general trends in the
international situation, the basic policy of the Ministry and the
particulars of the diplomatic activities of the Ministry.

Ministry of Education
    White Paper on Education (Kyoiku Hakusho) 1959 - Annual

Having a specific title for each year, as listed below, the paper
covers school education and education administration.

In an effort to provide objective reference material in order
to trace the history, identify problems and seek the means of
improvement in a particular area of education, a featured topic
is chosen from among school education, out-of-school education,
physical and health education, special education and education
administration for each year. Issues of 1959 and 1964 with the
title of "Educational Standards of Japan" may satisfy a general
interest to look at the situation of education in Japan.

    Topics -

    1959   - Educational standards of Japan

    1960   - Youth Education in a developing society

    1961   - Education in Remote and Isolated districts in Japan

    1962   - Development of the Nation and Education - Develop-
              ment of Education and Economic Progress

    1963   - Higher Education in Japan - Promotion of Higher
              Education in Postwar days

    1964   - Educational standards in Japan

    1965   - Social education in Japan - Situation and Problems

    1966   - Health and Physical Fitness of Youth

    1967   - Private Schools in Japan

Ministry of Health and Welfare
    Annual Report of Welfare Administration (Kosei Gyosei
    Nenji Hokoku) 1956 - Annual

Generally called the *Welfare White Paper*, occasionally having
an important issue as a sub-title, this White Paper usually
reports the year's activities of the Ministry in every field.

Consisting of two major parts, the first part being a general
description in order to outline trends of administration, to
explain the role, situation and problems of the Ministry and
finally to point out problems and to suggest the solution. In
the detailed exposition, an analysis of important areas of the
Ministry of Health and Welfare, and the reports of undertakings
are made.

The administration of the Ministry covers home life, the living
environment which is very important to each individual, and the
Japanese population. This report is therefore compiled in such
a manner that readers can gain a deeper understanding as to the
medical services, anti-pollution measures, recreation, the old
age pension system, social welfare, etc.

Environment Agency
    Annual Report on Pollution (Kogai no Jokyo ni Kansuru
    Nenji Hokoku) 1969 - Annual

Generally termed the *Pollution White Paper* it was submitted to
the Diet for the first time in 1969 according to Article 7,
Anti-Pollution Fundamental Law, in order to report the actual
situation of pollution in 1968 and to make public the suggested
programme to prevent pollution for the year of 1969. At first
the editing agency was the Ministry of Health and Welfare. The
so-called *Environment White Paper* has been published by the
Environment Agency since the issue of 1972.

Divided into 4 parts: Part I - Introduction; Part II - Situation
of Pollution; Part III - Measures taken to prevent pollution;
Part IV - Measures to be undertaken to prevent pollution for
1969.

In Part II, Analysis is made of air-pollution, water-pollution,
noise etc, based on data prepared by the Pollution Division of
the Ministry of Health and Welfare and other ministries. In
Part III, a report is made as to measures taken over each item

as mentioned in Part II. In Part IV, explanation is made as to
the establishment of environmental standards, the Planning of
the Pollution Prevention Programme, the promotion of other
measures to prevent pollution in general.

Ministry of Agriculture and Forestry
    Annual Report on Agricultural Tendencies (Nogyo no Doko ni
    kansuru Nenji Hokoku) 1961 - Annual

This is an *Agriculture White Paper* published exactly in the
same way as submitted to the Diet. "Agriculture Policies
suggested for the following year" which used to be published
separately has come to be attached, as an annex.

It is composed of 3 parts: Part I looks at agriculture for the
year in regard to productivity, standards of living; demand and
supply of agricultural products, and, management of farming.
Part II reports the outline of agricultural policies and Part
III suggests the projected agricultural policies for the following year.

Forestry Agency
    Annual Report of Trends in Forestry (Ringyo no Doko ni
    kansure Nenji Hokoku) 1964 - Annual

This is a *Forestry White Paper*, published as reported to the
Diet, with the inclusion of "Forestry policies to be suggested
for the next year".

Analysis is made in regard to forestry from such aspects as
national economy and forestry; demand and supply of forestry
products; forestry production, forestry management, and the
forestry labour force based on research and statistical data.
There are also reports of measures taken in the year and an outline of suggested measures for the following year taking into
account the result of analysis of tendencies in forestry evalu-
ation of the year's programmes.

Fishery Agency
    Annual Report of Trends in coastal fishery (Engan gyogyo no
    Doko ni kansuru Nenji Hokoku) 1963 - Annual

This is a *Fishery White Paper* published exactly as reported to

the Diet, with policies suggested for the year as to coastal
fishery in addition.

Detailed analysis is made as to the fishing economy, fishing
production, living standards of fishing households living on
coastal fisheries. Included in the report of measures taken
are: policies, legislation and financing for modernization and
rationalization of coastal fisheries. In the "suggested policies
for the following year", both traditional and new policies are
described.

Ministry of International Trade and Industry
    White Paper on International Trade (Tsusho Hakusho)
    1959 - Annual

A White Paper published mainly to review developments in international trade, under the title of *Situation of International
Trade in Japan* for the period of 1952-54 and under the title
International Trade White Paper ever since. Usually with a
sub-title for each issue.

Since 1958, the general outline and detailed exposition have
been separated into two volumes; the former viewing the historical background of international trade in Japan and problems and
perspectives of trade in the country's economy plus the development of the international economy; the latter describing in
detail the international balance of payments followed by
commodity-wise analysis, the country-wise trading situation,
and an outline of trading policies. Statistical data and charts
are fully used providing useful reference material.

Small and Medium Enterprise Agency
    Annual Report on Tendencies in Small and Medium Enterprise
    (Chusho kigyo no Doko ni kansuru Nenji Hokoku)
    1963 - Annual

The *Small Enterprise White Paper* published as reported to the
Diet based on the Small and Medium Enterprise Fundamental Law.
Also included are the "suggested policies of smaller enterprises
for the following year". A sub-title is designated for each
issue to show the central theme, such as "Small and Medium
Enterprise in an Internationalizing Era" in 1967, and "The Way
to a Developed Nation and Small and Medium Enterprise" in 1968.

It is composed of 4 parts, with the following contents: Part I:
general description of recent tendencies and the changing
economic environment; Part II: Analysis of recent tendencies
and identification of problems; Part III: A background of
policies taken, the basis for such measures, and reports of
policies undertaken; Part IV: Basic attitude and the content
of the suggested policies to be taken for the following year.

Ministry of Transport
    Annual Report of Transportation Economy (Unyu Keizai Nenji
    Hokoku) 1964 - Annual

It is commonly called the *Transportation White Paper* published
each year to report on the transportation economy.   Besides the
general report of the developments in the economy, each issue
features a special topic as named in the sub-title: "Transportation structure in the reformatory period" (1st), "Material
currency in the modernization process" (2nd), "Modernization
of transportation of the world and the direction of Japan"
(3rd), "Local economy and transportation structure" (4th),
"Solution urged for Traffic in big cities" (5th), "Changes in
progress of Transportation structure" (6th).

Identification of problems and direction suggested for solutions
regarding transportation and traffic safety are stated in the
general description.   An analytical exposition on transportation
economy for the year follows with regard to "land transportation", "Marine transportation", "air transportation",
"tourism" and "weather".

Ministry of Transport
    Situation of Marine Transport (Nippon Kaiun no Genjyo)
    1951 - Annual

The *Marine Transportation White Paper* first appeared in 1951
and was re-edited in the present form in 1955.

Part I is devoted to foreign-bound transportation and Part II
to inward-bound transportation.   Each part analyses the current
situation of marine transportation; describes how the marine
transportation policy is diffused, and points out future
problems.   Tendencies in world marine transportation and activities of Japanese outward-bound transportation are outlined in
Part I and problems of inward-bound transportation are pointed

out and explained in Part II.

Maritime Safety Agency
    Situation of Maritime Safety (Kaijo Hoan no Genjo)
    1951 - Annual

This is the *Maritime Safety White Paper* reporting shipwrecks
and rescues, marine traffic safety and prevention of damage in
coastal waters, and the administration of the Maritime Safety
Agency in regard to the maintenance of public order on the sea,
and requesting understanding and referring to necessary policies
to secure safety and further maintenance of order based on
analysis of the perils of the sea.

Ministry of Labour
    Analysis of Labour Economy (Rodo Keizai no Bunseki)
    1949 - Annual

This is a *Labour White Paper* started in 1945 with the *Analysis
of Post-War Labour Economy*. The general description deals with
an analysis of the dynamics of Labour economy and detailed
exposition further analyses the labour force, prices and wages,
and the income structure in relation to foreseen problems of
the future.

It is not, however, inclined towards the explanation of policies,
but tries to analyze the situation making full use of the comprehensive statistical materials on labour economy.

Ministry of Construction
    Current Situation of National Land Construction (Kokudo
    Kensetsu no Genkyo) 1948 - Annual

This is a *Construction White Paper* published annually in July
after reporting to the Cabinet during "Land Construction Week".

General remarks analyse the situation with regard to development
of land, land construction and new problem areas. Detailed
expositions in such fields as lands in Urban areas, housing,
roads, rivers, relate the current situation to the policy, and
analyse the tendencies of the construction business. Occasionally, reflections of land construction, and comparative analysis
on an international level, are made in order to analyse the

problem of land construction by a scientific approach taking
into account economic development and changes in the social
structure.

Ministry of Home Affairs
    Situation of Local Finance (Chiho Zaisei no Jokyo)
    1952 - Annually

The *Local Finance White Paper* is published by the Ministry of
Home Affairs as reported to the Diet and is based on the Local
Finance Act.

The current financial situation of the year of issue in local
government is analysed based on the statements of accounts submitted by prefectures municipal governments as well as towns
and villages. Other materials and problems are pointed out in
the general remarks. A comparison with the situation of the
previous year is also made. Finally, the prospects of the Local
Finance Plan for the next year is suggested on the basis of an
analysis of the current year. It is useful reference material
for the present situation including problems of finance of local
government.

The Fire Defense Agency
    Facts about Fires and the Current Situation of Fire Defense
    (Kasai no Jittai to Shobo no Genkyo) 1954 - Annual

It is a *Fire White Paper* analysing and explaining the situation
of fire damage and the abilities of fire defense. The White
Paper tries to analyse the degree of fulfillment in comparison
with the national standards, the defense administration, rescue
activities, finance, scientific studies on fire defense and
takes up problem areas which must be solved in the future.

CHAPTER 3
INVESTIGATIONS, STATISTICS, REPORTS, etc.

National Personnel Authority, Bureau of Compensation
    Situation of Wages in Private Sector - Survey on Wages
    by Occupation (Minkan Kyuyo no Jittai) 1948 - Annual

In compliance with Article 28 of the National Public Service
Act, the National Personnel Authority is obliged to report and
make suggestions regarding the level of compensation in the
public services to the Diet and the Cabinet.

To assess the optimum standards of wages, the Agency investigates
wage standards in the private sector. Started in 1948, this
occupation-wise situation is annually investigated and reported.

Areas of research include, the scale of enterprises, academic
background, sex, age and wage. The method taken has been
random sampling. The number of samples taken for the first time
was 391 enterprises from 25 types of occupation, involving 427
persons. This had increased to 6682 enterprises, of 19 types,
involving 446,005 persons in 1967. This is because the Agency
began to work in collaboration with the Personnel Committees
of prefectures and 5 big cities, in 1953, and this has been
continued up until today.

The result of the survey is published under the classification
of: scale of the enterprise, academic background, sex, age,
on national level as well as prefectural and 5 big cities levels.
Special professions such as teachers, doctors, nurses, are
covered, and wage basis, as well as allowance systems such as
bonuses, are also reported. It is often used by private
companies when deciding their wages.

National Personnel Authority
  Annual Report of National Personnel Authority([Jinji-in]
  Nenji Hokoku) 1948 - Annual

Ever since its establishment in December 1948, the National
Personnel Authority has been endeavouring to develop personnel
administration based on the modern idea to firmly establish a
democratic and efficient public service system in compliance
with the National Public Service Law, Laws relating to wages of
general workers, and Laws relating to the position classification
system of the public service. Article 24 of the National Public
Service Law describes the obligation of the Authority to report
their activities to the Diet and the Cabinet once a year, and
this is a publication of the report.

The activities of the Agency for the year are summed up under
headings of: Appointment and dismissal of staff members;
Wages of staff members; Service regulations; Disciplinary
measures; Efficiency; Compensation for accidents. Together
with the *20 years History of the National Personnel Authority*,
this report serves as good reference material in order to gain
a better understanding as to the changes in personnel administration in Japan.

The Prime Minister's Office,Office of Public Relations

  Current Situation of Public Polls on national level
  (Zenkoku Seron Chosa no Genkyo) 1953 - Annual

This is a directory of approximately 1,600 public polls conducted
by governmental offices, universities, institutions, private
enterprises - etc., on a nation-wide level during the year of
issue.

The main purpose is to obtain a complete picture of public polls
conducted and by so doing, to serve the convenience of the
public. Contents are: (1) Names of organizations associated
with public polls;(2) Situation of the public polls undertaken;
(3) Outcome of the polls.

The minimum requirement for inclusion is that the number of
respondents should be 300 or more, and that the questions asked
number more than 10, however, reported in this publication are
those with the ratio of 70% or more responses returned, or 500
or more responses obtained. Simple tabulations of major polls

are also attached. One can see the surveys and summaries of
outcome in this report. It is published by the Printing Bureau,
the Ministry of Finance under the title of *Public Poll Annual
Report.*

The Prime Minister's Office, Office of Public Relations
    Public Opinion Poll on Consciousness of Livelihood
    (Kokumin Seikatsu ni kansuru Seron Chosa?) 1948 - Irregular

This is one of the public opinion polls conducted by the Prime
Minister's Office. The latest of this kind is the 21st Poll in
May 1976.

The purpose is to investigate how people evaluate their present
life in order to obtain a clear idea about changes in
consciousness. 20,000 persons of 20 years old and more sampled
at random from every walk of life respond. Questions` posed are
related to (1) how they feel about their life; (2) their perspectives and hopes for the future; (3) their dissatisfactions in
life and demands for government action, and, (4) the raising of
children.

The outcome of the survey is published in about 50 pages with
statistical commentaries.

Prime Minister's Office, Statistics Bureau
    National Census (Kokusei Chosa) 1920 - every 5 years
    (Designated Statistics No. 1)

This survey is the largest in Japan. Commencing in 1920,
regular surveys have been conducted every 10 years and intermediate ones every 5 years, that is regular ones in 1920, 1930,
1940, 1950, 1960, 1970, and intermediate ones in 1925, 1935,
1947 (extra-ordinary), 1955, 1965, 1975. The one in 1975 was
the 12th census. In pre-war days, this was implemented by the
Statistics Bureau of the Cabinet in compliance with a law
concerning the National Census, but in post-war days the census
was appointed as Designated Statistics No. 1, based on the
Statistics Law. The main purpose of this survey is to make
clear the distribution of population by region, sex, industrial
and occupational structures, in order to provide fundamental
material for administration. Every person living at the time
of the census - 00:00 hour on October 1st, is included in the
survey.

Items included in the survey in 1970 were:

1) Name   2) relationship with the householder   3) sex   4) date
of birth   5) nationality   6) place of dwelling in the previous
year   7) educational background   8) marital status   9) years of
marriage   10) number of children   11) employment status   12)
working hours   13) name of employer   14) type of industry   15)
type of work   16) status in the work place   17) location of
work place (or school)   18) type of household   19) type of house
20) ownership of the house   21) number of TATAMI (mats for
living rooms) (dry grass - a unit for counting the width of a
room)   22) sources of income for households.

Japan is divided into 450,000 units with 50 households in a
unit and one researcher is appointed to each unit. The questionnaire is filled in by the head of each household and partially
by the researcher.

The Census has been regarded as the most important source of
population statistics and it later served as a basis for establishing the policies of each ministry. Although it once took
quite a long time for calculation and tabulation, it has been
increasingly shortened ever since the computer was introduced
in 1960. The benefits have been felt by both national and local
governments in terms of their need for the outcome of the survey.

Besides the results of population statistics being published,
results of other items are published in other forms.

Prime Minister's Office, Statistics Bureau, Economic Statistics
Division.
     Enterprises Statistical Research Report (Jigyosho Tokei
     Chosa Hokoku) 1947 - every 3 years (Designated Statistics
     No. 2)

This is said to have developed from a series of statistics
related to labour, such as the Labour Statistics Actuality
Report, Annual Labour Statistics Research, etc. conducted by
the Statistics Bureau of the Cabinet during the period from
1938 to 1946. The first survey, after separation from the
aforementioned reports, was conducted in 1947 and the second
one in the following year, and once again in the 3 years after-
wards. The purpose of this survey is to look into all the
enterprises in the country in order to know the distribution
and activities of enterprises in terms of district, type of
industry, and scale. The objects of investigation are all kinds

of business enterprises except farming, forestry, fishing
industries, and public services and occasionally peddlers, stall
keepers, kiosk keepers, etc. Included in the questionnaire are:
1) name   2) location   3) management structure   4) type of business   5) number of employees   6) distinction of head office
and branch office   7) Capital and Tangible fixed capital   8)
Amount of income and wages for service industry.

Except for the one published in 1948 under the title of *Findings
of Investigation of Wages of Enterprises*, the report has been
published under the present title.

Recently issues for "national level", "prefectural level",
"business enterprises", "service industries", "commentaries"
have been published separately. In addition, "Enterprises
Statistics Quick Release" is published for immediate use.

Prime Minister's Office, Statistics Bureau.
    Housing Statistics Survey (Jyutaku Tokei Chosa Hokoku)
    1948 - Every 5 years. (Designated Statistics No.14)

This was initiated in 1943 under the direction of the Allied
Forces, in order to understand the housing problems of post-
war days. The Housing Statistics have been compiled once every
5 years. According to the Statistics Law, it is appointed as
Designated Statistics No. 14.

The survey aims at clarifying the housing and habitation
environment. The method of survey is to interview samples from
both urban and rural areas, with more respondents in urban
areas. Average ratio of sampling is one eighth of the population throughout the country.

Questions asked are those about the house itself; 1) type of
house   2) family composition   3) structure of house and land
4) living conditions and background information about the
respondents, such as occupation and income.

Reports of the survey from Numbers 1 to 4 are published as a
monographic report and since the 5th survey in 1963, the report
has been published separately on a national and prefectural
level. This is the only material giving basic data on housing
conditions and problems in post-war days. As for the housing
in pre-war days, one item was included in the National Census
of 1930.

Prime Minister's Office, Statistics Bureau
   Labour Force Survey Report (Rodoryoku Chosa Hokoku)
   July 1947 - Monthly

The Survey on the Labour Force was begun in July 1947, and was
appointed as Designated Statistics No. 30 in April 1950.

The purpose of the survey is to understand employment and
unemployment, the structure of the employed population and its
dynamics. The subjects are 26,000 representative households
and 70,000 workers specifically for conditions of employment.
The survey is conducted during the last week of each month.
Items included for the employed are, employment, type of occupation, position in the work place, working hours, desire of
changing job, consciousness of work. Questions posed to the
unemployed are: desire of employment, preference for full-time
or part-time work.

Apart from this, *Annual Report of Labour Force* has been published
since 1963, being complimentary to the Labour Force Survey.
The *Extra-ordinary Labour Force Survey* has been conducted in
order to understand the working conditions and work consciousness as well as other facts about underemployment, and since
October 1953, reports of the survey have been published twice
yearly.

Prime Minister's Office, Statistics Bureau.
   Retail Prices Statistics Survey Report (Kouri Bukka Tokei
   Chosa Hokoku) June 1950 - Monthly

Started in June 1950 as Designated Statistics No. 35, this
survey aims at investigation of the retail prices of commodities, fares for public services, and house rents, obtained from
the shops and agencies, thus providing basic data for the
commodity price index, etc. Until June 1962, the survey was
conducted in 54 cities, 46 capital cities of prefectures and 8
other big cities, but was expanded to 172 cities, towns and
villages. Items for investigation include specified commodities,
house rents, public service fares, and school tuition which was
added in 1967.

This survey on which the calculation of average prices and the
price index is based, is most closely associated with the
standard of living of the people.

Prime Minister's Office, Statistics Bureau.
    Household Survey Annual (Kakei Chosa Nenpo) 1953 - Annual

Household surveys were conducted in 1926 and 1931 by the Statistics Bureau, the Cabinet before WWII. In post-war days, two
kinds of surveys "Consumer Price Survey" July 1946 - August
1950 and "Findings on Consumption" September 1950 - December
1952 were carried out, later to be integrated into the Household Survey Regulations (November 1st, 1952), and appointed as
the Designated Statistics No. 56.

The purpose of the Survey is to make clear the balance of payment
consumption, standards of living of households, and any dis-
parities between districts in order to provide basic data for
planning economic, social and other policies. Respondents of
approximately 4,200 households in 28 cities have been expanded
to 8,000 households in 170 cities, towns and villages since
January 1953. Besides background information about the respondents, questions are asked separately about Income and expenditure and detailed items of expenditure. During the time of a
dual price system, when controlled prices and black-market
prices were prevailing, the investigation of prices from the
consumer's point of view, instead of those from seller's side,
began in order to obtain a price index. In 1950, when the
economy of the country seemed to have stabilized, the question
on the income of a household was added to make the survey
complete. For those who would like to know more, a monthly
report can be referred to, which is published in addition to the
Annual report.

Another reference material is *Households in the decade after
WWII* which describes households during the period from 1946 -
1955, (with some re-arrangement in its presentation).

Prime Minister's Office, Statistics Bureau, Labour Force Statistics Division.
    Employment Structure Basic Survey Report (Shugyo Kozo Kihob
    Chosa Hokoku) 1956 - every 3 years (Designated Statistics
    No. 87)

This gives a clear picture of the employment, and unemployment
structure on both a national and district level. 250,000 households and all the family members above 15 years old in the household are sampled throughout the country according to a specific
method of questioning.

Besides the background information of the respondents, such
questions as; 1) type of work   2) desire and consciousness towards work   3) income   4) side-business   5) retirement - change
of work - re-employment during the year, are asked.

Except for the National Census, only this survey provides the
data of employment on the district level.

Recent issues are divided into "National" and "District", which
are then further sub-divided into several volumes.

Prime Minister's Office, Statistics Bureau, Consumption Statistics Division.
    Findings on Consumption in Japan, Survey Report (Zenkoku
    Sohi Jittai Chosa Hokoku) 1959 - every 5 years (Designated
    Statistics No. 97)

The aim of the survey is to make clear the income distribution,
standards and structure of consumption, and differences between
areas, by investigating household economies on a nation-wide
level.   About 30,000 households including single, but excluding
farming and fishing households are sampled.

Income and expenditure, kind of shops daily commodities are
bought from, possession of major durable commodities, family
members and the house are included in the questions.   Income
and expenditure usually refer to the housekeeping account books,
responses are filled in the questionnaire by the respondent as
to questions regarding durable goods, and questions regarding
the value of the family and house are asked by an interviewer.

The findings are tabulated both by prefecture and item, and
published accordingly.   For example, the reports in 1963 are
divided into 8 volumes: 1) Balance of Payment of Households
(National)   2) by locality - city, town, village   3) by prefecture   4) by city, town, village   5) by item   6) by the type of
shop   7) during commodity   8) explanation.

Prime Minister's Office, Statistics Bureau.
    Japanese Statistical Yearbook (Nippon Tokei Nenkan) No. 1,
    - 1882 - Annual

The *Japanese Imperial Statistical Annual* which had been published
59 times by the Statistics Institute of the Cabinet during a

period from 1882 to 1941, was re-published after WWII in 1949,
under the present title.

It contains comprehensive statistics compiled from major data
prepared by various ministries and other agencies concerned,
and includes details on land, weather, population, the labour
force, enterprises structure, agriculture, forestry, fisheries,
mining, manufacturing, construction, housing, electricity,
water supply, gas, transportation, communication, commerce,
trade, enterprise management, the currency, financing, prices,
wages, labour, social security, household education, culture,
religion, sanitation, the administration of justice, police,
calamities and accidents. Statistical charts show the changes
in figures from year to year. It is a highly regarded annual
with its accuracy and wide coverage.

Administration Management Bureau, Administration Management
Agency.
     Administrative Management Annual Report (Gyosei Kanri
     Nenpo) Vol. 1, 1950 - Irregular

This was initially published under the *Administration Structure
Annual Report* and since 1954 has been published under the
present title, principally on an annual basis. Although it has
not been regularly published as desired, the content is continuous. It deals with changes in national administration structure
and numbers of staff, in order to serve as reference material
for staff members of the agency and staff in charge of administrative management in other ministries and agencies. It also
provides the historical background information in regard to
administrative innovation.

Science and Technology Agency
     Annual Report of Science and Technology   (Kagaku Gijutsu
     Cho Nenpo) 1957 - Annual

The "Business Report on Promotion of Scientific Technology" of
the Agency published annually since its inception in 1956.

It is composed of 6 chapters: Chapter 1 outlining scientific
technology and major policies; Chapter 2 reporting the policies
undertaken during the year; Chapter 3 dealing with the activities
of attached institutions such as National Aerospace Laboratory,
Metallic Materials Technology Institute, National Research for

Disaster Prevention and so forth; Chapter 4 describing the
activities of consultative councils such as Council for Science
and Technology, Atomic Energy Commission; Chapter 5 reviewing
the activities of such agencies as the Japan Atomic Energy
Research Institute; Chapter 6 reporting activities within the
Agency. The style of editing has changed with Vol.12, to one
of separate general description and outlines of the policies
undertaken.

Science and Technology Agency
    Scientific Technology Researches Report (Kagaku Gijutsu
    Kenkyu Chosa Hokoku) 1953 - Annual (Designated Statistics
    No. 61)

This was originally named *Research Institutes Fundamental Statistics*, but was later changed to the present title in 1960 as
the scope of research was being expanded. The purpose is to
provide necessary information for the promotion of scientific
technology by clarifying the progress of scientific research.
Enterprises with capital of 1 million yen and more, institutes
and universities, etc. are included in the statistics. Since
1963, Technology Institutes have also been included. The method
utilized is filling in questionnaires sent by mail. All the
institutes and universities are included as respondents, while
a certain number of enterprises are sampled according to the
scale. Questions are about the number of employees, the quantity of research by speciality, total expenditure, and the
amount allocated to research. The number of respondents in 1965
was about 1,000 institutes and 1,200 universities, etc.

Results of the survey are reported by type of industry and by
scale for enterprises; by agency, discipline, the size of
researching staff for institutes; and by agency and by faculty
for universities, etc.

A quick report is published around December each year as an
intermediate report.

Ministry of Justice, Minister's Secretariat, Justice and Legislation Research Division.
    Correction Statistics Annual (Kyosei Tokei Nenpo)
    1948 - Annual

This is an Annual Report with a long history starting in 1903

under the title of the *First Annual Report of the Prison Bureau,
Ministry of Justice for 1890*, succeeded by the Execution Statistical Report in 1921, and then the present one in 1961. The
Correction of Juvenile Criminals Statistical Annual Report also
came to be published in 1953, but was terminated in 1960, when
the two publications were integrated into the *Correction Statistics Annual*.

Statistical reports of criminals are taken in prisons, Boys'
prisons, detention houses, Boys' Reformatory School, Juvenile
Classification offices, Women's Guidance Homes, in the fiscal
year. It is one of the few sources of statistics in the field
of correction of criminals.

Ministry of Foreign Affairs
    Japan's Diplomatic Correspondence (Nippon Gaiko Bunsho)
    Vol. 1 - 1868   The United Nations Association in Japan

This is a collection of records of diplomatic correspondence
kept by the Ministry. Preparation started in 1935, and the
first publication appeared in the following year. Vol. 45 No. 1
issued in 1963 marks the end of the Meiji Era, and major diplomatic incidents and general history are presented.

A book of each volume is principally devoted to the collection
of diplomatic correspondence for the year, and separate books
are published for major incidents. For diplomatic correspon-
dences after the Meiji Era, the "Chronological Table of Japan's
Diplomacy and major correspondence between 1849 and 1945" edited
by the Correspondence Section, the Ministry of Foreign Affairs
(published by UN Assn.) which embraces the records of correspondence until the end of WWII could be referred to. For the post-
war period, the "Collection of Public Announcements of the
Ministry of Foreign Affairs", produced by the Public Information
and Cultural Affairs Bureau, as a bi-annual (six months) publication makes useful reference material.

General Affairs Division, National Tax Administration Agency
    Facts about Wages in Private Sectors - Findings of Survey
    on Wages in Private Sector (Minkan Kyuyo no Jittai)
    1947 - Annual (Designated Statistics No. 77 since 1954)

The survey is conducted each year in order to find out the
standards of salaries and wages in the private sector. It was

implemented by the Tax Bureau of the Ministry of Finance but they were then replaced by the Tax Administration Agency from the second year onwards.

The survey aims at clarifying the levels of income according to Income-level classification, scale of enterprise, type of occupation, scale of company, in order to get basic data for taxation administration, including an assessment of the amount of taxes for the year. Those who are covered in this survey are salaried workers, except government servants and day labourers sampled out of those in charge of collection of tax at the source, and salaried workers. Samples are taken in 3 stages out of the Taxation Office, enterprises and salaried workers.

The difference between this survey and the one by the National Personnel Agency lies in the fact that this provides the basic data for levying tax, and is characterized by its ability to present income-level distribution and facts about smaller enterprises, as well as facts about salaries according to the scale of enterprises, etc.

National Tax Administration Agency, Director's Secretariat, General Affairs Division.
    Annual Statistical Report of Taxation Agency (Kokuzei - Cho Tokei Nenposho) 1874 - Annual

Ever since it was published for the first time in 1874, the report has been providing basic data on domestic taxes.

Self-assessment, levy, collection of domestic taxes and other related items are shown so that the structure of taxation in regard to how many tax payers paid their taxes and how the amount of the tax is calculated could be clarified. No special survey is conducted for this report, and the data is collected from among what the Agency already has for their work. All of the tax payers of 30 and more kinds of industries are covered, and samples out of major taxation items - self-assessed income tax, tax at the source, enterprise tax, are dealt with.

Charts are categorized by: General, the Direct National Tax, the Indirect National Tax, and collection of tax, and direct and indirect taxes are arranged by tax classification.

This satisfies the increased interest in recent years in tax, and it provides important data to understand economic tendencies from the point of view of tax.

Ministry of Education, Minister's Secretariat, Research and
Statistics Division.
     Fundamental Report on Schools (Gakko Kihon Chosa Hokoku)
     1951 - Annual (Designated Statistics No. 13, 1948)

Appointed as the Designated Statistics No. 13, in 1948, this
survey is annually implemented. However, this could date back
to 1873 when "Annual Report of the Ministry of Education" came
into existence. The report is one of the basic reference
materials separated from the Ministry's Annual Report in which
"school" related chapters were included.

The purpose of this survey is to obtain fundamental data on
school education and education administration in every field of
school education as described in the School Education Act such
as numbers of students, schools, classes, theatre, teachers,
correspondence courses, out-of-school students, school facilities, school expenditure, attached facilities, including the
library and students' post-graduation life. The survey ranges
from kindergarten to universities with the emphasis on primary,
secondary and tertiary levels. Statistical charts as of 1st of
May each year are presented with several pages of explanation.

Ministry of Education, Minister's Secretariat, Research and Statistics Division.
     Report on School Teachers (Gakko Kyoin Chosa Hokokusho)
     1947 - every 3 years (Designated Statistics No. 9)

This was appointed as the Designated Statistics No. 9, as the
first one published by the Ministry of Education.

With the purpose of obtaining basic information in order to plan
teacher training, re-education within the work place, and working
conditions and investigating backgrounds, length of service,
amount of salary and working attitude of every teacher employed
by the Ministry of Education including principals, teachers,
nursing teachers, nursing assistant teachers, lecturers of
primary, secondary, tertiary schools and schools for the blind,
for the deaf and other schools for the disabled; and presidents,
professors, associate professors, lecturers and assistants of
universities and junior colleges.

Questions covered since the first issue in 1947 are academic
backgrounds, working attitude, length of service, amount of
salary, type of teaching licence, hours of teaching per week.

Reports are occasionally divided into two: one covering primary
to tertiary education and the other covering junior colleges
and universities.

It initially served mainly the GHQ of the Allied Forces, and
was used for the training of teachers according to the revised
school system. At present it helps with the problems of re-
education of teachers in order to meet the new needs of
education.

Ministry of Education, Minister's Secretariat, Research and
Statistics Division.
    Annual Report of Ministry of Education (Mombusho Nenpo)
    No. 1 - 1873 - Annual

This is a comprehensive report of education administration published since 1875 (of 1873 fiscal year). Occasionally having
"Japan" or "Japan Imperial" on top of the title. Mimeographed
complementary reports for the missing period from 1938 to 1948
were published during 1959-61 (No. 66 - 76).

The editing policy was drastically changed by the 79th issue of
1951 from one which recorded the work of the ministry and fundamental statistics of school education to a report of major statistics, and a fundamental report on schools which came to be
published separately. The present report is composed of
"outline", "materials" and "statistics". "Outline" reviews
the works of the ministry, "materials" report important legislation and notifications.., "statistics" show the outcome of
various surveys. Information is given as to basic data on the
Ministry's administration education system, education statistics
and other educational affairs since the Meiji Era.

Ministry of Education.
    80 Years Chronological History of Education (Gakusei 80
    nenshi) 1954, 1222 p. The Printing Bureau, Ministry of
    Finance.

This traces 80 years development in school education after the
promulgation of the school system in 1872. Focussing on the

system, it is composed of two parts: the commentary and the reference material. A chronological explanation of the history and development of education is made in the text, the decade of drastic changes after WWII being commented upon in particular detail in several pages.

In the section of "reference materials", educational regulations and instruction orders from GHQ, the summarized report of the 1st and 2nd educational mission to the USA, a Chart of the school system, statistics of education, and a chronological table of school education are included.

The *90 years Chronological History of Education* published in 1963 also describes the history of education, with major emphasis placed on the past decade referring only in part to the preceeding decades.

Ministry of Education.
  70 years Chronology of Industrial Education (Sangyo Kyoiku 70 Nenshi) 1956, 1152 p.

This is a detailed review of industrial education of the Meiji (1848 - 1911) Taisho (1912 - 1925), and Showa (1926 -) Eras, centering on the system and administration and covering education in agriculture, industry, commerce, fishing, home economics, and vocational guidance. Chapters of explanation and reference material compose this book, later published as the *50 years chronology of practical Education*, with emphasis on the period during and after WWII.

Complementary to this is the *80 year chronology of Industrial Education* (published in 1966, p. 736), which describes the industrial education of the country in two parts - pre-war and post-war, with major emphasis on the 20 years after WWII.

Ministry of Education.
  90 Years Chronology of Kindergarten Education (Yochien Kyoiku 90 Nenshi) 1969, 785 p.

90 Years of Kindergarten education from its inception in Tokyo Women's Teachers Training College as its attached institution in November 1876, are outlined in 2 parts; explanatory description and reference materials. It covers:

1) 90 years chronological table,

2) Education regulations,

3) Notification, annual report of the Ministry, journal of the ministry,

4) Education statistics.

Articles and items related to kindergarten education are subsequently described in 2), 3) and 4).

Ministry of Health and Welfare, Minister's Secretariat, Research and Statistics Division.
    Population Dynamics Statistics (Jinko Dotai Tokei)
    1946 - Annual

This is a report of population dynamics by year which aggregates the monthly reported figures. It was formerly published by the Statistics Bureau of the Cabinet. Important statistics have been continuously published, from the *Population Dynamic Statistics of 1899* (Published in 1902) till today, except for a few years towards the end of WWII before the responsible agency was shifted to the Ministry of Health and Welfare in September, 1947 (report for 1946 fiscal year).

Japanese births, deaths, marriages and divorces are tabulated so that the dynamic phenomenon of people could be seen in a continuous manner. The mode of survey is by reports submitted by chiefs of municipalities, town and village governments, based on the Population Dynamics Research Act, for population movements, on the Census Registration Act for births, deaths, marriages, and divorces, and on regulations regarding stillborn child delivery. This report provides important data as an indication of standards of health and sanitation as well as culture, and serves interested people in such fields as population problems, education planning, social welfare policy making. After 1951, it has been published in two separate volumes, the previous ones having had an irregular style.

The *Population Dynamics Statistics Monthly Figures* are also published.

Ministry of Health and Welfare, Minister's Secretariat, Statistics and Research Division.
    Survey on Social Medical Service (Shakai Iryo Chosa Hokoku)

1955 - Annual (Designated Statistics No. 79)

This has been annually published since the 1st survey in 1955.
The purpose of the survey is to make clear the illnesses and
medical treatment for which medical insurance is paid. 70,000
cases are sampled out of "Claims for Medical service fees" submitted by hospitals and clinics throughout the country.

Questions are asked as to the type of illness, the number of
medical consultations, points, days of services, which are
covered by medical insurance and the life protection law.

A report is compiled of facts about the sick and the wounded,
medical treatments, and statistical tables and charts. It was
published as the "Social Medical Service Research Annual" until
1959.

Information on problems of medical insurance in general based
on social insurance can be obtained.

Ministry of Health and Welfare, Minister's Secretariat, Statistics and Researches Division.
    Sanitation Administration Business Report (Eisei Gyosei
    Gyomu Hokoku) 1960 - Annual

A report successively published with the *Sanitation Annual Report*
(of 1941 - 59), a part of which was separated, this report
becoming an independent publication. Other parts include the
Dominant Character Protection Statistical Report. The origin
of this report dates back to the *Sanitation Bureau Annual Report*
published since 1877 by Sanitation Bureau, Ministry of Home
Affairs.

The title of the *Sanitation Annual Report* came to be used in
1937 when the editing and publishing responsibility was shifted
to the Ministry of Health and Welfare. The aim of this report
is to provide fundamental data for systematic and rational
management of sanitation administration by understanding the
actual situation of the administration with reports of work
submitted by prefectural and specified cities. Therefore, the
subjects of the survey are departments and divisions concerned
with health and sanitation in the above mentioned local governments. Responses to the prescribed items are reported by
persons in charge of the local government. These responses are
reported monthly, quarterly and then annually. 70 tables in

total are published under such items as mental hygiene, nutrition, isolated treatment of epidemics, VD, sanitation
inspection, environmental sanitation, food sanitation, milk and
meat sanitation, X-ray, medical services, masseurs, acupunctur-
ists, dental sanitation, health nurses, midwives, medical nurses,
pharmacy, hot springs.

It provides indispenable reference material which can be used
to trace the history of public hygiene and health after the
Meiji Restoration, having undergone major transition during the
emergency period of the late WWII, and total change right after
WWII to meet the needs of a new era. The *Dominant Character
Protection Statistics* should be referred to along with this
report.

Ministry of Health and Welfare, Minister's Secretariat, Statistics and Research Division.
    Business Report of Social Welfare Administration (Shakai
    Fukushi Gyosei Gyomu Hokoku) 1960 - Annual

The former *Social Welfare Statistic Annual* which had been published during 1951 - 55, 1956 - 59 was terminated in 1959, and
this was separated into 3 independent reports in 1960; the
*Business report of Social Welfare Administration, Livelihood
Protection Dynamics Report; Facts about social welfare
institutions.*

The aim of this survey is to obtain information necessary for
better administration of social welfare through quantitative
comprehension of prefectural administration after the enforcement of regulations relating to Social Welfare (e.g. Livelihood
Protection Act, Child Welfare Act, etc.), recording list of
children and the other reports submitted by all the institutions
to the prescribed questionnaire. Welfare offices, Children's
counselling centres, Women's counselling centres and other social
welfare facilities, throughout the country are covered. Livelihood protection, rehabilitation of the physically handicapped,
welfare of the aged and the mentally retarded, public pawnshops,
women's protection, the social welfare commissioner, welfare
funds for the one-parent family, child welfare, children's
allowances, special assistance for the war-sick and war-wounded,
and other items, are included in the report.

Statistics are made public four times a year: monthly, quarterly,
bi-annually and annually. Important articles are usually

reported in the monthly publication of the same kind.

Ministry of Agriculture and Forestry, Statistical Information
Department.
    Comprehensive Statistics on Agricultural Household Economy
    (Noka Keizai Sogo Tokei) 1949 - Annual (Designated Stat-
    istics No. 36)

The aim of the survey is to grasp the changes in the agricultural structure and the tendencies in the agricultural economy
as well as the position of agriculture in the national economy
by looking at the management of individual farming households.
55,000 full-time farming households are sampled.

References to the account books and interviews are used in order
to ascertain the facts about cash and material dealings according
to items of expenditure, increase and/or decrease of assets.

The report of the result is published in 11 separate books since
1962 by prefecture, by social rank, by social stratum and by
national level.

An overall picture could be found in the comprehensive report.

No. 1)   Comprehensive Statistics of Agricultural Households

No. 2)   Value Statistics of Agricultural Households

No. 3)   Asset Statistics of Agricultural Households

No. 4)   Capital dynamic Statistics of Agricultural Households

No. 5)   Living Expenses Statistics of Agricultural Households

No. 6)   Nutrition Statistics of Farmers

No. 7)   Economic Statistics of Agricultural Households by type
         of household

No. 8)   Economic Statistics of Agricultural Households by
         economic sector

No. 9)   Taxation, levy and other responsibilities of Agricul-
         tural Households

No.10)   Labour Statistics of Agricultural Households

No.11)   Statistics pertinent to the commercialization of agricul-
         tural products

No.12)   Statistics pertinent to the utilization of Agricultural

Cooperatives by Agricultural Households.

Ministry of Agriculture and Forestry, Statistical Information
Department.
   Statistical Table of Ministry of Agriculture and Forestry
   (Norinsho Tokeihyo) 1st issue - 1924 - Annual

This is a Statistical Table with a long history which began with
the *Statistics Table of Ministry of Agriculture and Commerce*
No. 1 to No. 40 (1884 - 1923). The latest one, No. 51 of (1950-
51) is the 91st.

Fundamental statistics on Agriculture and Forestry, prepared
mainly by the Statistics and Research Division of the Ministry
with some additions from other sections and agencies are compiled
in 20 sections including Agricultural Households, Farming Land,
Agricultural Products, Forestry, Fishery, etc. A systematic
presentation of statistics with a commentary is made in every
section, and figures of the preceding 5 years are shown in
addition.

The *Ministry of Agriculture and Forestry Statistics Cumulative
Table* also provides useful material (for 1868 - 1953).

Ministry of Agriculture and Forestry, Minister's Secretariat,
Administrative Division.
   Annual Report of Ministry of Agriculture and Forestry
   (Norinsho Nenpo) 1953 - Annual

This was published in 1953 under this title after the *Agriculture
and Forestry Yearbook* (1950-53), and the *Agriculture Yearbook*
(1948-49).

It is principally an annual report of the Ministry's administration, outlining the position in agriculture, forestry and the
fishing industries for the year, together with the policies of
the Ministry. The general description reviews the administration
and the detailed exposition relates to the policies undertaken
by the Bureaux in the Ministry and the activities of extra-
departmental bodies. A Directory of related legislation-
enactments, abolition and amendment is attached. This is the
basic information on the process of administration of the
Ministry. The *History of Agriculture and Forestry Administration* by the Ministry also serves an an important reference material.

Ministry of Agriculture and Forestry, Statistical Information
Department.
    World Census of Agriculture and Forestry (Sekai Noringyo
    Census) 1950 - every 10 years

This provides fundamental agricultural statistics. The Census
was given the present name to participate in the World Agriculture Census (1950) initiated by FAO. Although the FAO's World
Census is conducted once in every 10 years, the Ministry imple-
ments an intermediate survey every 5 years. This has developed
from the General Survey of Agricultural Households (1938), the
first survey of census type, followed by the *Agriculture
Fundamental Survey* in 1941, the *Population Survey of Agricultural
Households* (1946), the *Extraordinary Agriculture Census* (1947)
and by the *World Census of Agriculture and Forestry* in 1950.
The *Census on Agriculture and Forestry* and the *Extraordinary
Agriculture Fundamental Survey* for 1955 were carried out on the
basis of the Designated Statistics No. 26 and 75 respectively.

This census is composed of 4 surveys:

A survey of agricultural households, a survey of large scale
agricultural households, a survey of farming villages, and a
survey on cooperative management bodies. The 1st survey covers
the number of family members, and various factors in agricultural production; the second one covers those with incomes
amounting to 1 million yen or more, in order to differentiate
these from self-employed farming households; the 3rd one
investigates the possession of farming machines on a mutual
basis, and the living environment of the village.

The results are reported by 4 different surveys and by prefecture. Listed below are the titles of the report in the recent
census and the intermediate census.

World Census 1960

        Statistical Table by city-town-village (46 Vol.)

        Statistical Table of Forestry District Survey (46 Vol.)

        Agriculture in Japan

        Report of Agricultural Households

                Households and Population

                Means of Production

                Fruit

        Agricultural Product-Selling Households (I) and (II)

        Sampled Tabulation (I) and (II)

Report of Farming Villages

Reports on Forestry

Report on Habitual Mutual Possession

Report by Agriculture district, economic activity districts

Report of Economic Activity Districts

Post-Survey Report

English version of the report

1965 Agriculture Census

        Statistics Table on prefectural level (56 Vol.)

        Report of Agricultural Households

        Report of Large Scale Farming Households

        Report of Cooperative Management

        Report by Agricultural Districts, Economic Districts

        Report of Sampled Agricultural Households

Food Agency

    Food Control Statistics Annual Report (Shokuryo Kanri Tokei Nenpo) 1948 - Annual

This is a statistical report on food-related surveys conducted by the Food Agency during the fiscal year. Production, Price, Inspection, Demand and Supply, Manufacturing, Transportation, Storage, Accounting of the main crops of Japan such as rice and barley, etc; and statistics on the food situation in other countries are systematically compiled. An example is fundamental data such as the list of government purchase prices for (1946 - 1969) and the list of government sales prices.

It is indispensable reference material for those in charge of food control, food administration, scholars interested in food problems and the general public as well.

Ministry of International Trade and Industry, Minister's
Secretariat, Research and Statistics Department.
    50 Years Chronology of Industrial Statistics (Kogyo Tokei
    50 Nenshi)   The Printing Bureau, The Ministry of Finance.
    1961-13, 3 vol.

Industrial statistics were begun in 1883 with the *Factory Statistics* conducted according to the Notification No. 21 of the
Ministry of Agriculture and Commerce, but one can go further
back to the *Production Survey* in 1870 by the Ministry of People's
Affairs (Minbu sho) which partially dealt with a survey of this
kind.

50 years of industrial statistics are reviewed, including, above
all, the statistics which were kept unpublicised as the "top-
secret militaristic information". Reference Book I covers
statistical tables by type of industry; Reference Book II by
items; the third one presents the transition of industry in
Japan by industry, by scale of industry, by district, and there
is a general explanation as well.

Ministry of International Trade and Industry, Minister's
Secretariat, Research and Statistics Department.
    Industrial Statistical Table (Kogyo Tokeihyo) 1939 - Annual

This is a collection of statistical tables of the Survey on
Industrial Statistics (the Designated Statistics No. 10). It
dates back to the *Factory Statistics Table*, in 1909, which was
published once in 5 years until 1919 and annually from then on.
The title changed to the present one in 1925. It was unpublished
in 1943 and 1944. The purpose of the survey is to make the
industrial situation clear. The method is the filling in of the
questionnaire by respondents who are manufacturers listed in the
Standard Industry Classification in Japan.

Examples of questions are:

(1)   scale and form of management

(2)   amount of products delivered

(3)   raw materials

(4)   electricity consumption

(5)   total amount of wages, etc. which covers the management of
      an enterprise generally

The results of the survey are published as follows:

- Industrial statistical table (industry) in which responding enterprises are classified by manufacturing activities and the results are presented according to the classification
- Industrial statistical table (article) in which results are presented by manufactures and articles
- Industrial statistical table (enterprise) in which the results are presented by type of industry, this is actually a re-arrangement of the "industry" section
- Industrial statistical table (Land and water service)

Recently, editions for enterprise and water service are published as separate volumes.

The *Industrial Statistics Quick Report* is published in addition for speedy release.

Ministry of International Trade and Industry, Minister's Secretariat, Research and Statistics Department.
     Textile Statistics Annual Report (Seni Tokei Nenpo)
     1953 - Annual   (Designated Statistics No. 19)

The range of the survey covers all the sectors of the industry, synthetic fibres, spinning textile fabrics, etc.

All of the manufacturers were included in the survey for the initial period, but now only samples are taken. Contents include: indices of production/delivery/stocks; transition of employees; production facilities; raw materials; marketing and international trade statistics.

Ministry of International Trade and Industry, Minister's Secretariat, Research and Statistics Department.
     Commerce Statistics Table (Shogyo Tokei hyo)
     1952 - Bi-annual (2 years)   (Designated Statistics No. 23)

This is a report of Statistics of Commerce implemented bi-annually since 1952. All the shops classified as wholesaler and retailer by the Standard Industry Classification are asked to fill in 3 kinds of questionnaires. Questions posed relate to the number of employees, sales by month and year, the amount of merchandise in stock; service charges and intermediary charges, and space for sales.

This could be regarded as a "Commerce Census" in Japan and provides precious fundamental data covering all of the shops within the country. It is presented in 3 volumes: vol. 1 - *Industry*, vol. 2 - *prefecture*, and vol. 3 - *items of merchandise*.

Ministry of International Trade and Industry, Minister's Secretariat. Research and Statistics Department.
    Machines Statistics Annual Report (Kikai Tokei Nenpo)
    1952 - Annual

This is an annual report summarising the *Monthly Report of Statistics of Machines and Tools Marketing* (the Designated Statistics No. 101) and the *Machines Statistics Monthly Report* as well as pertinent sections of the *Production Dynamic Statistics* (the Designated Statistics No. 11).

The Production Dynamic Statistics are limited to enterprises with 20 or more employees. Though not all articles are covered, major machines and tools are included, as well as the processes of production, delivery, production capacity, raw materials and personnel management. Production statistics, machines and tools, marketing statistics and reference materials therefore make up this report.

Ministry of Postal Services
    Annual Statistical Report of the Ministry of Postal Services
    (Yubin Tokei Nenpo) 1953 - Annual

This is an annual report of the statistics of services such as the telephone, the telegram, the mail, money order savings, and insurance, etc. by which the work of each section can be understood. Besides this, a monthly report is published.

Being separated according to duties; the *General Remarks* reviews the general work of the Accounting and Finance Bureau, and the Mailing service of the Postal Bureau, others are the *Telecommunication Service* by the Postal Bureau, the *Money Order Savings* by the Savings Bureau, and the *Insurance and Pensions* by the Post Office Insurance Bureau.

Ministry of Labour, Minister's Secretariat, Statistics and
Information Department.
    Labour Statistics Monthly Report (Maitsuki Kinro Tokei
    Chosa Kekka Hokoku) 1944 - Monthly   (Designated Statistics
    No. 7)

This was started in 1944 by the Statistics Bureau of the Cabinet
according to the Labour Statistics Regulation, and was appointed
Designated Statistics No. 7 in 1947 upon enforcement of the
Statistics Law. In 1951 the duty was transferred to the Ministry
of Labour.

The roots of this kind of survey could, however, be found in the
Monthly Survey on Wages of Workmen and the *Monthly Survey on
Wages of Mine Workers* implemented by the social Bureau of the
Ministry of Home Affairs since 1923, and the *Monthly Survey of
Wages* which has later been carried out by the Statistics Bureau
of the Cabinet. This is one of the traditional surveys in Japan.

The main purpose is to discover the monthly changes in employment, wages, working hours, number of working days, on both a
national and prefectural level. Samples of public and private
enterprises having 30 or more employees regularly (sometimes 5
or more workers) are chosen by district as well as by scale of
the enterprise.

Reports on the national level and the local level have been
published on a separate basis since 1951.

Minister of Labour, Minister's Secretariat, Statistics and
Information Department.
    Comprehensive Report of Monthly Survey on Labour (Maitsuki
    Kinro Tokei Chosa Sogo Hokokusho) 1961 - Annual

This is a summarised annual report of both national and local
levels. Changes in the year are presented by tables and charts.
It has been published since 1961.

Ministry of Labour, Minister's Secretariat, Statistics and
Information Department.
    Report of Survey on Wages of Outdoor Workers by Type of
    Occupation (Okugai Rodosha Shokushu-betsu Chingin Chosa
    Hokoku) 1948 - Annual   (Designated Statistics No. 53)

This started with the *Survey on Wages of Day Labourers* in 1948, and has been published ever since, although there have been changes in title. It was appointed as Designated Statistics No. 53 in 1952.

The purpose of the survey is to obtain fundamental data on the working conditions of day labourers in the construction and land, harbour and port transportation industries. Respondents are private enterprises with more than 10 full-time employees (5 for construction) in 27 types of sub-classified industries of the construction industry; 8 kinds of industries in harbour and port transportation, and 6 kinds of industries in land transportation.

The scale of the company, type of industry, form of employment, sex, form of wage, working hours, days of working, the amount of wage, etc., are inquired into. The result is reported by prefecture and by type of industry.

Ministry of Labour, Statistics and Information Department.
    Report of Wage Structure Fundamental Statistics (Chingin
    Kozo Kihon Tokei Chosa) 1954 - Annual (Designated Stat-
    istics No. 94)

Fully-fledged surveys have been conducted in 1954, 1958, 1961, 1964, 1967 and supplementary ones each year, thus bridging these gaps. The purpose of this survey is to understand the situation in regard to wages of full-time employees of major industries.

900,000 respondents are sampled by a certain ratio among groups of enterprises classified by scale. The survey is carried out by staff members of the Labour Standards Office of each prefecture and by those of the Labour Standards Supervising Office. Type of industry, region, the size of enterprise, type of employees, sex, type of occupation, type of employment, academic careers, age, years of employment, years of experience, days of working, hours of working, and wages are made clear by this survey.

It is regularly published providing important information on the wage system. Associated information can be obtained in the *Report of the Comprehensive Survey on Wages* published in 1961 by the Research and Statistics Division of the Minister's Secretariat, the Ministry of Labour. 13 volumes, appendix, 5 volumes on prefectural level.

Ministry of Labour, Minister's Secretariat, Statistics and
Information Department.
   Labour Statistics Annual Report (Rodo Tokei Nenpo) 1948 –
   Annual

This was called the *Labour Statistics Survey Annual Report* until
1952, and then changed to the present title.

Fundamental data on labour economy and the current labour situation and its changes are provided to assist in understanding
labour problems. Statistical data is available from the
Division as well as labour statistics of foreign countries and
those of concerned sections of other ministries.

Statistical tables collected in this report are: the Labour
economy index, working hours, salaries, employment and unemployment, accidents, labour productivity, the cost of living, labour
unions, labour disputes, and international labour statistics.
It provides comprehensive material giving basic data on labour
problems with the additional convenience of a written explanation in English.

River Bureau, Ministry of Construction.
   Floods Statistics (Suigai Tokei) 1961 – Annual

This is a report of the recognized surveys based on the Statistics Report and Researches Act carried out since 1961.

The purpose of this survey is to obtain basic data on the amount
of damage caused by floods during the fiscal year on a regional
basis. Rivers and other causes are looked at in order to plan
the counter-measures. Calamities included are: floods, high
tide, tidal waves, mud and stone flows and land slides. Data
on damage to assets is included, general assets such as houses,
household appliances, redemption assets, goods in stock,
agricultural products, and public infra-structures such as
rivers, roads, ports, urban structures and water supply
facilities.

Tables of the amount of damage are arranged by prefecture level,
and city-town-village level, and by climatic causes, sources of
rivers, rivers and shores. Besides the amount of damage, the
quantity is also shown.

Ministry of Home Affairs, Local Administration Bureau.
   Survey of Compensation of Local Government Workers (Chiho
   Komuin Kyuyo Jittai Chosa) 1955 - every 5 years
   (Designated Statistics No. 76)

Commencing in 1955 as Designated Statistics No. 76, it was
conducted once every 5 years after 1958. The latest one on 1st
April, 1973 is the 5th. This survey is intended to clarify
payment of government workers in order to re-evaluate the wages
system of the local government. All of the workers employed by
local government except for school teachers are asked questions
regarding age, sex, academic career, months of employment, job
classification and position, amount of salary.

The number of employees, the amount of salary and other allowances are classified by employment agency, financial allocation,
job classification, years of employment, academic career and
age group.

Board of Audit.
   Report of Audit of Settlement of Account (Kessan Kensa
   Hokoku) 1890 - Annual

This is the report of audit by the Board of Audit, which is
obliged to inspect the balance of payments of the government
according to Article 90 of the National Constitution. It serves
as an official document for Parliamentary deliberations on the
settlement of accounts. The Cabinet submits this report together with the settlement of accounts to the Diet of the
following year. Therefore, the audit of the settlement of the
accounts is the most important task of the Board. Since the
first report the "Audit of Income and Expenditure" for 1886
fiscal year, published in 1890, this report has been continuously
published.

The contents of the report are arranged according to Article 29
of the Board of Audit Law, and Settlement of Income and Expenditure, confirmation of settlement, comparison of the amount of
settlement with that submitted by the Bank of Japan, expenditures
from reserved funds without Parliamentary consent, unlawful
conduct and suggestions for correction, suggestions for improvement of laws, systems and administration, etc. are included.

APPENDICES

1. Agreement Concerning the Treatment of Government
   Publications (White Paper, etc.)   185

2. Regulations of the Council for the Diffusion of
   Government Publications   188

3. Agreement of the Council for the Diffusion of
   Government Publications   191

4. List of the Designated Statistics   194

IJGP - N

Appendix 1.

Agreement Concerning the Treatment of Government
Publications. (White Paper, etc.)

(Agreement of the Council of the Permanent Vice-
Ministers, on 24th October, 1963)

Among the government publications that each ministry and agency
compile, the white paper, etc. (whose definition is described
in the note), has been successfully playing a role in deepening
the recognition of the public for the actual state of politics,
economics and society and for the present condition of government policy, and in supplying much important and valuable
material. However, as there seem to be some problems with
regard to the content, etc., of white papers, the following
improvements should be made.

1.   As the white paper, etc., is principally intended to
       make the public aware of the actual state of politics,
       economics and society, the prospect for the future and
       the course of policy (hereinafter referred to as "the
       prospect for the future, etc.") shall be mentioned
       incidentally.

2.   When referring to the prospects for the future, etc.,
       it shall be described most generally and abstractly,
       especially when referring to matters concerning the
       important policy of the government, and unless other-
       wise officially agreed as government opinion, the consent
       of the Cabinet Council shall be obtained in advance.

3.   In order to establish the authority for compiling and
       publishing the white paper, etc.,

       (1) Regarding the white paper, etc., of the annexed
            list: It shall be compiled under the name of each
            ministry and agency and the effects shall be made
            clear in the preamble. It shall be published after
            reporting or distributing to the Cabinet Council
            and finally being approved. However, in the case
            of a publication which is a report submitted to the
            Diet based on the law, it shall not need to obtain

a consent from the Cabinet Council.

The official press release shall take place after the end of the Cabinet Council Meeting, and when giving the press the white paper, etc., for pre-announcement, it shall be so arranged that the press will release it after the official announcement.

(2) As for other white papers other than the above: They shall be compiled under the responsibility of the director of bureau or a higher person in each ministry and agency and the effect shall be made clear in the preamble, also in regard to publishing. Depending upon the importance of the white paper, etc., concerned, it shall obtain consent from the ministry, permanent vice-minister or the director of the external bureau.

4. Among the Government publications, the ones which may use the word "white paper" as their official title (including the sub-title) shall be limited to those in the annexed list.

Concerning the printing and publishing of the white paper, etc., in accordance with the stipulations of "the Council of Reinforcement for Diffusion of Government Publications" (understanding of the Cabinet Council, on 2nd November, 1956), the Printing Bureau of the Ministry of Finance shall, in particular, be utilized.

5. In taking the above measures, for practical effect, each party concerned shall keep in contact with each other through "the Council for Diffusion of Government Publications" (established in conformity with the aforementioned understanding of the Cabinet Council) which is based in the Prime Minister's Office.

Also, when planning to publish new white papers (including non-periodicals) in each ministry and agency, the same shall be applied. (With the consent of the Cabinet Council, the publications that may be called white paper could be added.)

(Note):

The white paper, etc., mentioned above shall be furnished with the following requisites:

(1) They shall be government publications which are compiled by national government offices. (According to the above-

mentioned understanding of the Cabinet Council, a government publication is "the printed matter which is compiled by a government organization and sold or distributed").

However,

a. Material compiled or written under an individual name with official status shall be excluded.

b. The inter-departmental materials shall be excluded, though "not-for-sale" ones which are widely distributed shall be included.

c. It shall be limited to book form alone, and in principle monthly magazines and pamphlets, etc., shall be excluded.

(2) Its main purpose shall be to make the public aware of the actual state of politics, economics and society and the present condition of government policy.

Therefore, the explanatory book of laws and regulations, etc., the mere reports of statistics research and introductory books on the work of existing government offices shall be excluded.

Appendix 2.

Regulations of the Council for the Diffusion of
Government Publications

(Decision of the Council for the Diffusion of
Government Publications on 30th November, 1956)

1. The Council for the Diffusion of Government Publications
(hereinafter referred to as "the Council") shall be
established in the Prime Minister's Office.

2. The Council shall be composed of the officials concerned
in each ministry and agency (including the Legislation
Bureau and the National Personnel Authority) who are
assigned by the Prime Minister.

3. The Council shall deliberate on the following matters:

   (1) Matters concerning the publication of Government
   publications.

   (2) Matters concerning the management of the Service
   Center for Government Publications.

   (3) Matters concerning the diffusion of Government
   publications.

4. The Council shall compile the Government Publications
Catalogue on the basis of the materials in item 7.

5. The Council shall have a chairman. The Director of the
Inquiry Commission shall be appointed the chairman.

   The chairman shall preside over the Council.

   In a case of the chairman suffering an accident, the
   member who was appointed in advance by the chairman shall
   take over.

6. Council' meetings shall in principle be held once a month.
However, if necessary, a special meeting shall be held.

7. Members of the Council shall notify the council in
advance of the documents, among the materials of each
department and bureau concerned (including the external
bureaux and the government relating organizations), which

188

they found it proper to sell to the public as Government
publications, and shall submit about 50 copies of Government publications and the like, which are not intended
to be sold, to the Council.

8.   In suitable cases any party concerned from an agency or
        other government related organization, other than the
        members of the council, shall obtain the chairman's
        consent and shall participate in the Council meeting and
        take part in the proceedings.

9.   The Council shall have a subcommittee if necessary.

10.   When deciding matters concerning the specific ministry
        or agency (including government related organizations)
        in the proceedings of the Council or sub-committee
        meeting, the approval of the ministry and agency con-
        cerned shall be obtained.

11.   The general affairs of the Council shall be transacted
        in the Inquiry Commission of the Prime Minister's
        Secretariat.

Regulations of the Council for the Diffusion of Government
Publications   (Amended on 10th July, 1963)

1.   The Council for the Diffusion of Government Publications
        (hereinafter referred to as "the Council") shall be
        established in the Prime Minister's Office.

2.   The Council shall be composed of the officials concerned
        in each ministry and agency (including the Cabinet
        Legislation Bureau and the National Personnel Authority)
        who are assigned by the Prime Minister.

3.   The Council shall deliberate on the following matters:

        (1) Matters concerning the publication of Government
             publications.

        (2) Matters concerning the management of the Service
             Center for Government Publications.

        (3) Matters concerning the diffusion of Government
             Publications.

4.   The Council shall have a chairman. The Director of the
        Office of Public Relations shall be appointed as chair-
        man.

        The chairman shall preside over the Council.

In the case of an accident to the chairman, the member
who was appointed in advance by the chairman shall take
control.

5.   The Council meeting shall in principle be held once a
month. However, if necessary, a special meeting shall
be held.

6.   In suitable cases, any party concerned from any agency
or other government relating organizations, other than
the members of the council, shall obtain the chairman's
consent and shall participate in the council meeting and
take part in the proceedings.

7.   The Council shall have a subcommittee if necessary.

8.   When deciding matters concerning specific ministries and
agencies (including the government related organizations)
in the proceedings of the Council or sub-committee
meeting, the approval of the ministry or agency concerned
shall be obtained.

9.   The general affairs of the Council shall be transacted
in the Office of Public Relations of the Prime Minister's
Secretariat.

Appendix 3.

Agreement of the Council for the Diffusion of
Government Publications

(Decision of the Council of the Diffusion on 18th
December, 1956)

Concerning the management, etc., of the Council for the Diffusion
of Government Publications (hereinafter referred to as "the
Council"), the following was agreed upon:

1.   With regard to the reinforcement for the diffusion of
      Government publications (the decision of the Cabinet
      Council on 2nd November, 1956), as for paragraph 4, II.,
      2. Publication of Government Publications, the following
      shall be excluded in principle:

      (1) Periodicals which have been published by the same
           publisher.

      (2) Publications which need specific techniques, etc.,
           and ones which are held to be better suited to
           private publication.

2.   Details which are to be notified, as for Item 7 of the
      Regulations of the Diffusion of Government Publications,
      shall be as follows:

           title of the book, name of the compiler, form and
           pages scheduled date of publication, expected
           numbers of the publication and outline of the content.

3.   If the above-mentioned notification submitted to the
      Council is very urgent, the Council shall deliberate on
      it in collaboration with the ministry and agency concerned
      and with the Printing Bureau.

4.   Treatment of government publications and other materials
      (hereinafter referred to as "publications, etc.") which
      are reported or submitted to the Council for the purpose
      of preparing the Catalogue of Government Publications
      shall be as follows:

(1) The scope of the publications, etc., reported or
     submitted to the council.

     A.   In principle the ones which are compiled or
          prepared by the national government offices
          shall be included.

     B.   In regard to the publications not on the market,
          only ones which do not cause public discussion
          when published shall be included.

(2) The report of the publications, etc., for the month
     accompanied by a certain number of copies shall be
     submitted to the chairman of the Council by the
     fifth of the following month according to the speci-
     fied form (Government Publications Report).

Agreement of the Council for the Diffusion of Government
Publications

(Amended on 10th July, 1963)

Concerning the management, etc., of the Council for the Diffusion
of Government Publications (hereinafter referred to as "the
Council"), amending the agreement decided on 18th December, 1956,
the following was agreed upon:

1.   A member of the Council shall notify the Council in
     advance of the publications, which are proved to be
     appropriate for publishing as government publications.
     The publications are from among the materials of each
     department and bureau concerned (including the external
     bureaux and the government relating organizations).
     Details of the notification shall be as follows:

          title of the book, name of the compiler, form and
          pages, scheduled date of publication, expected
          numbers of the publication, outline of the content
          and expected price.

2.   A member of the council shall submit the government
     publications and other materials (possibly fifty copies),
     which are not for sale and are prepared by each department
     and bureau concerned (including the external bureaux and
     the government relating organizations), to the Council
     for general distribution.

3.   A member of the council shall present the report necessary
     for the preparation of the Catalogue of Government

Publications as follows:

(1) The report for every month shall be presented to
     the chairman of the Council by the first day of the
     following month.

(2) It shall be made according to the specified form
     (Government Publications Report).

(3) It shall be accompanied by three copies each of the
     publication (including two copies for display at
     the Service Center).

However, the copies need not be presented if the publication is expensive.

With regard to the reinforcement for the diffusion of
Government publications (the understanding of the Cabinet
Council on 2nd November, 1956), as for paragraph 4, II.,
2. Publication of Government Publications, the following
shall be excluded in principle:

(1) Periodicals which have been published by the same
     publisher.

(2) Publications which need specific techniques, etc.,
     and ones which are held to be better suited to
     private publication.

Appendix 4. List of the Designated Statistics

Designated No.	Title	Government Agency
1	National Cabinet	Statistics Bureau, the Cabinet
2	Enterprises Statistics	Statistics Bureau, the Cabinet
3	Research on Agriculture, Forestry, Fishing Industries	Ministry of Agriculture and Forestry
4	Research on House Lot System	Agency for Rehabilitation of Post War
5	Vital Statistics - Research on Population Movement	Minister of Health and Welfare
6	Research on Ports and Harbours	Minister of Transport
7	Monthly Report of Labour	Minister of Labour
8	Day time Population of Tokyo Metropolis	Governor of Tokyo Metropolis
9	Report on School Teachers	Minister of Education
10	Industrial Statistics	Minister of Commerce and Industry
11	Production Dynamic Statistics	Minister of Commerce and Industry
12	Inhabitants Statistics of 1948	Director of Statistics, Prime Minister's Office
13	Report of School	Minister of Education
14	Housing Statistics	Director of Statistics, Prime Minister's Office
15	Statistical Report of Health of School Children	Minister of Education
16	Report on Fishing Rights	Minister of Agriculture and Forestry
17	Monthly Report of Seamen's Labour Force	Director of Statistics, Prime Minister's Office
18	Livestock Census in 1949	Minister of Agriculture and Forestry
19	Statistics on Textile Marketing	Minister of Commerce and Industry

194

20	Statistics on Farming Land in 1949	Minister of Agriculture and Forestry
21	Statistics on Shipwrecks	Minister of Transport
22	Special Survey on Consumer Price	Director of Statistics Bureau, Prime Minister's Office
23	Statistics on Commerce	Minister of International Trade and Industry
23	Statistics on Commerce of Aomori Prefecture	Governor of Aomori Prefecture
24	Statistics on Effective Price of Producer's Goods	Director General Economic Consultation Agency
25	Survey on Population in Hokkaido	Governor of Hokkaido Prefecture
26	Census on Agriculture and Forestry	Minister of Agriculture and Forestry
27	Dynamic Statistics on Demand and Supply of Coal, etc.	Minister of International Trade and Industry
28	Statistics on Ships and Seamen	Minister of Transport
29	Statistical Report on Shipbuilding and Machine Building	Minister of Transport
30	Survey on Labour Force	Director of Statistics Bureau, Prime Minister's Office
31	Statistical Report of Mined Coal and its quality	Minister of Resource Agency
32	Statistics on Construction initiated	Minister of Construction
33	Survey on Livestock Products	Minister of Agriculture and Forestry
34	Statistics on Sales of Department Stores	Minister of International Trade and Industry
35	Statistics on Retail Prices	Director of Statistics Bureau, Prime Minister's Office
36	Survey on Farming Households Economics	Minister of Agriculture and Forestry
37	Survey on Products	Minister of Agriculture and Forestry
38	Report on Sericulture and Cocoon Products	Minister of Agriculture and Forestry
39	Dynamic Statistics on Agriculture	Minister of Agriculture and Forestry
40	Statistics on Quality of Metal Mining	Minister of International Trade and Industry

Designated No.	Title	Government Agency
41	Survey on Situation of Utility of Forests	Minister of Agriculture and Forestry
42	Statistics on International Tourism	Minister of Transport
43	Dynamic Statistics of Products of Gas	Minister of International Trade and Industry
44	Population Census of TAMASHIMA CHO	Mayor of TAMASHIMA Town
45	Population Census of NAKATSUGAWA CHO	Mayor of NAKATSUGAWA Town
46	Statistical Survey on Machines, Tools and Equipments	Ministers of International Trade and Industry, Transport, Welfare
47	Survey on Industrial Education	Minister of Education
48	Dynamic Statistics on Production of Medical Industry	Minister of Health and Welfare
49	Dynamic Statistics on Demand and Supply of Non-Iron Metals	Minister of International Trade and Industry
50	Population Census in YANAGAWA CHO	Mayor of YANAGAWA Town
51	Dynamic Statistics of Demand and Supply of Oil Products	Minister of International Trade and Industry, Minister of Transport
52	Survey of Population of TOSHIMA Village, Oshima County, Kagoshima Prefecture	Director, Statistics Bureau, Prime Minister's Office
53	Survey on Wages of Outdoor Workers according to the type of work	Minister of Labour
54	Statistics of Haul of the Oceanic Fishery	Ministry of Agriculture and Forestry
55	Statistics of Labour Productivity	Minister of Labour, Minister of International Trade in Industry
56	Survey on Households	Director of Statistics Bureau, Prime Minister's Office
57	Survey on the Economy of Private Enterprises	Director of Statistic Bureau, Prime Minister's Office
58	Dynamic Statistics of Trading Companies	Minister of International Trade and Industry
59	Urgent Fundamental Survey on Seri-culture	Minister of Agriculture and Forestry
60	Fundamental Survey on Welfare Administration	Minister of Health and Welfare

61	Research Survey on Scientific Technology	Director of Statistics Bureau, Prime Minister's Office
62	Survey on Demand and Supply of School Teachers	Minister of Education
63	Survey on Day-Time Population of HIROSHIMA City	Mayor of HIROSHIMA
64	Dynamic Statistics of Commerce	Minister of International Trade and Industry
65	Report on Medical Service Facilities	Minister of Health and Welfare
66	Survey on Patients	Minister of Health and Welfare
67	Fishery Census	Minister of Agriculture and Forestry
68	Survey on Health of Japanese	Minister of Health and Welfare
69	Statistics on Lumber	Minister of Agriculture and Forestry
70	Statistics of Population in Amami Islands	Prime Minister
71	Dynamic Statistics of Productions of Railway Vehicles, etc.	Minister of Transport
72	Survey on Wages of Individual Workers	Minister of Labour
73	Basic Findings on Wages according to the type of work	Minister of Labour
74	Survey on School Facilities	Minister of School
75	Extraordinary Fundamental Survey on Agriculture for 1955	Minister of Agriculture and Forestry
76	Survey on the Salary of Workers in the Local Government	Minister of Home Affairs
77	Facts about Wages in Private Sectors	Director-General of National Tax Administration Agency
78	Fundamental Survey on Agriculture and Fishing in Amami Islands	Minister of Agriculture and Forestry
79	Survey on Social Medical Services	Minister of Health and Welfare
80	Survey of Employment by District, etc.	Minister of Labour

Designated No.	Title	Government Agency
81	Survey on Assets of Corporated Enterprises in preparation for the National Wealth Research in 1965	Director-General of Economic Consultation Agency
82	Survey on School Lunches	Minister of Education
83	Survey on Social Education	Minister of Education
84	Statistics of Construction	Minister of Construction
85	Survey on Assets of Private Enterprises in preparation for the National Wealth Research of 1965	Director-General of Economic Planning Agency
86	Survey on Assets of Households in preparation for the National Wealth Research of 1965	Prime Minister
87	Basic Survey on the Employment Structure	Prime Minister
88	Fundamental Findings on Labourers in the Small and Medium Sized Enterprises	Minister of Labour
89	Survey on Assets of Public Enterprises run by Local Authorities in preparation for the National Wealth Research in 1965	Director-General of Economic Planning Agency
90	Statistics of the Seamen's Labour Force	Minister of Transport
91	Statistical Survey on Investments of Incorporated Enterprises	Director-General of Economic Planning Agency
92	Urgent Livestock Census	Minister of Agriculture and Forestry
93	Comprehensive Fundamental Survey on Smaller Enterprises	Minister of International Trade and Industry
94	Fundamental Statistics on Wage System	Minister of Labour
95	Statistics of Paper Marketing	Minister of International Trade and Industry
96	Extra-ordinary Survey on Coastal Fishery	Minister of Agriculture and Forestry
97	Findings on Consumption in Japan	Prime Minister
98	Fundamental Findings of Commerce in Japan	Minister of International Trade and Industry

Page	Title	Source
99	Statistics of Transportation of Automobiles	Minister of Transport
100	Statistics of Rice Production Cost	Minister of Agriculture and Forestry
101	Statistics of Machines and Tools Marketing	Minister of International Trade and Industry
102	Basic Findings of Fruit Trees in 1963	Minister of Agriculture and Forestry
103	Report on Transportation Service by Coastwise Vessels	Minister of Transport
104	Population Census of KADOMA Cho	Mayor of KADOMA Cho
104	Population Census of HIGASHI MURAYAMA Cho	Mayor of HIGASHI MURAYAMA Town
104	Population Census of HINO Machi	Mayor of HINO Town
104	Population Census of KOKUBUNJI Cho	Mayor of KOKUBUNJI Town
105	Comprehensive Survey on Livelihood in 1966	Minister of Health and Welfare
106	Comprehensive Survey on Food Consumption in 1966	Minister of Agriculture and Forestry
107	Population Census of MESASAGI Cho	Mayor of MISASAGI Town
107	Population Census of NAGAREYAMA Cho	Mayor of NAGAREYAMA Town
107	Population Census of YACHIYO Machi	Mayor of YACHIYO Town
107	Population Census of HATOGAYA Cho	Mayor of HATOGAYA Town
108	Report of Commodity Prices in Japan in 1967	Prime Minister

INDEX

Administrative Management
    Agency   70
Admiralty Hydrographic
    Department, U.K.   87
Agriculture White Paper   149
Amended Treaty of Rome   72
Arisawa, H.   72
Arita, K.   117
Atomic Energy Commission
    Monthly Report   133
Atomic Power White Paper   146

*Basic Finding of Changes in
    People's Living
    Standards*   145
Bern Treaty   72
*Bibliography of Government
    Publications*   119
Biblos   120
Board of Audit   182
Bureau of the Official
    Gazette   9
Bureau of Typewriting   92

Cabinet Council   105
Catalogue of Books   89
*Catalogue of Books of the
    Government
    Organizations*   119
Central Office of Information,
    U.K.   87
Central Public Relations
    Organization   49, 53
Chugai Newspaper   7
Commentary   14, 56, 96
*Commentary-Window of the
    Government*   131

Commerce Statistics Table   177
Compilations   75
Construction White Paper   152
Copyright   77
    term of protection   79
Copyright Catalogue   15
Correction Statistics Annual
    163
*Council for the Diffusion of
    Government Publications*
    188, 191
Council of Special Libraries
    109
*Chronology of Practical
    Education*   168
*Current Movement; A Window of
    the Government*   56, 95
Current Topics Review   94

Deposit Copy System   107
Deposit Copy Weekly   119
Designated statistics list   194
Designated statistics system
    65
Dore, R. P.   102

Economic Planning Agency   38,
    143
Educational Standards in Japan
    147
Educational Statistics   135
*Employment Structure Basic
    Survey Report*   160
Encyclopaedia   5
Encyclopaedia of Allied Works
    5
Entrusted Works   75

Environment White Paper 148
Escarpit, R. 106
Europeanization 4, 10
Exhibition of Government
    Publications 106

Factory Statistics 176
Fair Trade Commission 143
Fire White Paper 153
Fishing White Paper 149
Floods Statistics 181
Food Agency 175
Forestry White Paper 149

*General Catalogue of Government
    Publications and Others*
    126
Government Organizations,
    works of 73
Government Printing Office,
    U.S.A. 87
Government Publications
  agreement concerning the
      treatment of 185
  annotations of 127
  characteristics 30
  copyright 72
  diffusion and enforcement
      members 91
  definitions 22
  distribution 98
  General Bibliography 119
  history 3
  National Service Centres
      100
  periodicals 130
  production procedure 45
  publication in Europe
      and U.S. 85
  publicity media 55
  publishing 88
  regulations of the Council
      for the Diffusion of
      188, 191

  retrieval 117
  sales organization 100
  services for users 110
  statistical viewpoint 16
  treatment of 185
  types 27
  uses 18
  white papers 35, 142
*Government Publications
    Newspaper* 125
Government Public Relations 48
Government statistics 58
Government structure 24
Gunshoruiju 5

Her Majesty's Stationery
    Office, U.K. 86
History of statistics in
    Japan 72
Household Survey Annual 160

Ide, Y. 52
Imperial Bulletin 3
Imperialism 6
Imperial Library 109
Inai, K. 112
Industrial Statistical Table
    176
*International Trade White
    Paper* 150
Ishibashi 102
Ishii, G. 91

*Japanese Imperial Statistical
    Annual* 161
Japanese National Bibliography
    120
Japan Statistical Institute 70
Japan Statistical Yearbook 16
Journal of the Cabinet 3, 6

Kamiide, H. 81

Keiji era 5
Kidera, S. 121
Kondo, K. 97, 112
Kono, I. 37
Kuroki, T. 26, 34, 92, 112,
    121

Labour Force Survey 159
Labour Statistics Annual
    Report 181
Labour Statistics Monthly
    Report 179
Labour White Paper 152
Library of Congress 110
Local Finance White Paper 153

Machines Statistics Annual
    Report 178
*Marine Transportation White
    Paper* 151
Maritime Safety White Paper
    152
Meiji era 4
Meiji government 93
Mijata, H. 23
Ministries, Bureaux of 122
Ministry of Agriculture and
    Forestry reports 172
Ministry of Education 72, 80
  Annual Reports 166
  Federation of Social
    Education 96
  magazines 134
  Social Education Bureau 96
Ministry of Finance Printing
    Bureau 78, 89, 92
Ministry of Foreign Affairs
    109
Ministry of Foreign Affairs
    Researches Monthly
    Report 133
Monopoly White Paper 36,
    143
*Monthly Catalogue of
    Government Publications*
    120, 125

Mori, S. 112
Murakami, K. 3

National Census 156
National Diet Library 90, 111
National Diet Library Law 23,
    108
National Personnel Authority
    154
National Population Census 6
Newspapers, commercial 4
Nishizaki, M. 99, 112
Nisshi, D. 3
Notified statistics system 68

Office of Public Relations 54
Official Bulletin 3
Official Duty Works 75
Official Gazette 4, 6, 7, 9,
    14
Official Gazette Commentary 96
Official Publications 22
Okada, N. 113
Okuma 8, 9
Oll'e, J. G. 92
Ordinance Survey, U.K. 87
Otsuki, F. 5
Outline of Geography 5

Paper Money Office 92
Patent Office, U.K. 87
Periodicals 130
Personnel Directory 94
Photo 56, 131
Photograph Weekly 95
Political speeches 74
Pollution White Paper 148
Population Dynamics Statistics
    169
Post Bureau 100
Printing Bureau of the
    Ministry of Finance 92
Printing Bureau Publications
    78, 95

Private newspaper 8
Promulgation Ordinance 12
Publication Catalogue 126
Publicity media 55
Public Polls 155
Public relations in
     government 48, 50

Radio broadcasting 56
Radio Wave Review 138
Report Control Act 70
*Report of the Actual Conditions
     of the Economy* 36
*Research on Government
     Publications* 18
*Retail Prices Statistics
     Survey Report* 159
Rice's Report 62

Saito, T. 112
Sakuma, N. 26
Sakurai, Y. 112
Sanjo, S. 7
Sanitation Annual Report 170
Sano, B. 81
Schmeckebier, L. F. 92
Scientific Technology Agency
     133, 145, 162
Service Centres 103, 105
Shiina, R. 46
Showa era 6
Small Enterprise White Paper
     150
Social Education 96
Statistical organization 62
Statistical Reports
     Coordination Law 70
Statistical research 58
Statistical system in Japan 60
Statistics Law 62
Statute Book 93
Sugai, K. 112
Suwaraya, M. 3
Suzuki, T. 81

Suzuki, Y. 17

Taisho era 6
Tanabe, Y. 25, 34, 91
Taxation Agency 165
Television broadcasting 56
Term of protection 79
Textile Statistics Annual
     Report 177
*The Fifth White Paper on
     Health and Welfare* 37
Tokyo Daily Newspaper 7
Tourism White Paper 142
Trade Bibliographies 124
Transportation White Paper
     151
Tsuchiya 95

Uchida, M. 5
Ueno Library 107
Utsumi, K. 72

Wages 180
Weekly Review of Events 94
Welfare White Paper 148
White Papers 35, 39, 142,
     185
White Paper on Crime 146
*White Paper on International
     Trade* 36
*White Paper on National Living
     for 1968* 38
Works of Government
     organizations,
     exploitation of 77
World Agriculture Census 174
World Economic White Paper 144

Yamagata, A. 7
Yamamoto, K. 81
Yamashita, N. 113
Yamauchi, K. 27, 34

DOES NOT
CIRCULATE